Deconstructing Your Faith without Losing Yourself

Deconstructing Your Faith without Losing Yourself

Angela J. Herrington

William B. Eerdmans Publishing Company
Grand Rapids, Michigan

Wm. B. Eerdmans Publishing Co.
4035 Park East Court SE, Grand Rapids, Michigan 49546
www.eerdmans.com

Published 2024

Book design by Lydia Hall

Printed in the United States of America

30 29 28 27 26 25 24   1 2 3 4 5 6 7

ISBN 978-0-8028-8328-5

Library of Congress Cataloging-in-Publication Data

A catalog record for this book is available from the Library of Congress.

To my guy: Hell or high water, here we are
and I wouldn't have it any other way.

To my babies: Each of you is a gift
and I will never get tired of your laughter.

To the strong women who came before me:
Your legacy of compassion reminds me to love generously
and help someone when I can.

Contents

Foreword

What's so important and helpful about Angela's book is how it fits into the historical context of what's called the deconstruction movement.

I checked back in my blog, *Naked Pastor* (nakedpastor.com), and discovered that the first time I used the word "deconstruction" was in 2006. I had co-opted it from the French philosopher Jacques Derrida, whom I was reading at the time. The word and its meaning, as far as I could understand it, provided what I thought was a perfect description of what I was experiencing spiritually at the time: a thorough and devastating questioning of my beliefs and faith.

Even though people would comment, accusing me of being nothing but a deconstructionist, I didn't take it as an insult, as they intended, but as a compliment.

It confirmed to me that I was onto something. I continued using the word to describe what I was experiencing. I felt very alone in my deconstruction journey because it had enormous ramifications for my church life and for my blogging life.

My blog was where I was sharing my story, and eventually I got found out. This ultimately led to me leaving the ministry and, therefore, the church, in 2010. I would have stayed, but I knew the church wasn't the safest place for questioning everything.

However, I came to find out that I was going through a process that others were experiencing as well.

In response to this rising awareness, and realizing the blatant absence of resources for people who were in the process of deconstruction, in 2012 I started creating material as well as an online community with the express purpose of providing a safe space and resources for people who were going through this process.

Up to that point, I think the options for questioning our beliefs were down to two: (1) to keep it to yourself so that you could continue belonging to the church community or (2) to express your questions and risk alienation and maybe even expulsion from the community.

With the decline of the authority of the church and religion in general, and their power over our lives, more and more people were willing to take this risk and question their beliefs, no matter the consequences.

At the same time, others were noticing the gap as well and started filling it with more resources and groups.

The concept of deconstructing our beliefs was becoming commonplace. It was being normalized and validated across the world. I was happy to see the growing awareness of what I believe is a normal and healthy aspect of human and spiritual growth.

This is why I love Angela's book and appreciate its importance right now.

She not only provides one of the most thorough outlines of what deconstruction is but also outlines the diverse ways of dealing with it in our personal lives.

I imagine Angela as a kind of coach for an explorer. She provides what tools you might need, prepares you for the dangers you may face, and describes what you may discover on your journey. She refuses to take you where you think you should go—because she doesn't know! All she knows is that this is your journey, you're the pioneer, and you're the only one who can find your new home.

Because it is different for everybody.

Like I always say: There's only one way to deconstruct—your way!

So, if you're questioning your beliefs or your relationship to religion or the church, this book is kind of a manual for preparation before you embark on the deconstruction journey and an encouragement for while you're experiencing it.

For many, it might be more like light being shed on what you already went through. Ah! So that's what happened!

It's obvious Angela experienced, and experiences still, deconstruction herself. We both agree that deconstruction is a way of life. And she shares the wisdom she's gleaned from her journey with all those who are on a similar pilgrimage.

We are not going crazy.

We are not alone.

We will all find our own way.

We will find our own spiritual home.

And we will all be better for it.

David Hayward

INTRODUCTION

Deconstruction Is Not a Trend

I'm not here to save your faith, protect the church, or convince you that a specific set of Christian beliefs is the one and only path to God.

Contrary to what you may have heard from critics of deconstruction, I'm also not here to abolish the church, create anarchy, or lure you into abandoning your faith altogether and embracing atheism.

Deconstruction isn't about selectively asking questions approved by your faith community while avoiding challenges to the core doctrines your belief system is built upon. That would just be learning how to fit into a different religious system than the one you are currently wrestling with. Instead, it's an exercise in examining your beliefs about God, faith, spiritual practices, and religious community. Deconstruction isn't a ten-step formula that is easily passed from one person to another. It's a very personal journey that is shaped by your beliefs, experiences, privilege, and traumas.

The purpose of this book, and everything else I do as a faith deconstruction coach, is to create a sacred space for the vulnerable exploration of what you believe. I'm here to offer you tools and processes that empower your exploration, expand your view of what's possible, and celebrate your ability to make your own choices about what you want to believe.

The Sophia Society is an online community dedicated to supporting deconstructors and hosts the *Holy Heretics* podcast. Contributor Melanie Mudge describes deconstruction as "the taking apart of an idea, practice, tradition, belief, or system into smaller components in order to examine their foundation, truthfulness, usefulness, and impact."[1]

Deconstruction invites us to become really honest about what we believe, why we hold these beliefs as sacred, how they influence the way we relate to our Creator, and who is *actually* served by our beliefs. If we trust the process enough to lower our walls and honestly engage with our questions, deconstruction promises to reveal undiscovered bias, limiting beliefs, and any flawed doctrines that actively harm people.

How can I say with certainty that those things are present in the majority of a Christian's personal beliefs? Because Christianity has been connected to corrupt power, genocide, and white supremacy for centuries. Even though the universal Christian church has splintered into hundreds, perhaps thousands, of sects and denominations, we all trace our roots back to the same early Christians left to manage Jesus's legacy after his execution more than two thousand years ago. People in the early church may have begun as underdogs and outsiders, but it didn't take long for powerful political leaders to weave Christianity into their quests for ever-increasing influence.

The modern Bible translations, doctrines, creeds, and sacraments that many Christians hold as perfect and unchallengeable were also used to justify genocide, forced conversion, chattel slavery, Manifest Destiny, and other horrific injustices. It is unfathomable to assume that these abusive practices could fade away on their own when they are so deeply rooted in American cultural and spiritual identities. It's also difficult to believe that Christians could have spearheaded such harmful movements without their bias and corrupt motives influencing the church as well.

Christianity has both shaped and been shaped by corrupt, abusive beliefs about the inherent value of people and resources. Faith deconstruction is a tool you can use to peel back each layer of corruption to determine what's at the core of your beliefs. Sometimes, there's nothing sacred or holy to find. A belief is not worth keeping. So you grieve, make amends, and toss that belief out. Other times you may find a spark of the Divine buried under centuries of bad doctrine, and you can diligently peel back layer after layer until the Truth is revealed.

Deconstruction is an essential season of moving *away* from toxic, man-made religion and moving *toward* the wild, sacred, and holy Creator of all things.

Faith deconstruction requires a tremendous amount of vulnerability and courage because the religious systems that raised us also taught us not to question. We were raised to believe that some thoughts, ideas, and questions were off-limits because they challenged the foundational doctrines of those faith communities. They threatened to shift the power balance away from the centuries-old structure built upon gender bias, misogyny, colonialism, and white supremacy.

Instead of cultivating independence and autonomy in believers, the majority of religious systems cultivate dependence upon the community. Assimilation into the beliefs and culture of the majority within the faith community is the goal, not the spiritual flourishing of individual members. These toxic religious systems have grown even more powerful by weaponizing the human need for connection and belonging to threaten those who get "too curious" with rejection from the community.

Anyone who has ever been overly inquisitive in a small group or Christian book club knows exactly how that weaponized need for belonging feels. Other group members withdraw visibly when you cross the well-defined line in the sand that delineates which questions are acceptable. Your willingness to ask such a question threatens your position as a trusted and welcomed member of a faith community.

I've been there and, because you're reading this, I have a hunch you've been there too. It stings. Many of my clients describe feeling as if they have asked one too many questions and that those questions are out of bounds or have gone too far. The fear of abandonment is embedded in our DNA. When we look around the room at people we deeply trust and see them recoil from our most intimate questions and fears, there is an immediate desire to get out. Sometimes we wish we could take it back; other times, we wish we'd never trusted this community enough to open up in the first place. Either way, the pressure to never let it happen again is tremendous.

So what do we do? Most of us push those doubts back into the corners of our brains and lean into what the community believes. Maybe we don't really believe it now, but we tell ourselves that it's our human weaknesses and lack of faith that are creating the gap between what we believe and what our community says we *should* believe. We turn inward, criticize ourselves for our perceived shortcomings, try harder, and gradually become more critical of ourselves while becoming less critical of our unhealthy faith community. Why? Because that's exactly what we've been conditioned to do. Assimilation and compliance uphold the existing system and punish those who challenge it, even if that system *needs* to be challenged for its own well-being.

In this book you'll learn that deconstruction is the antidote to toxic religion's conditioning and pressure to assimilate. My goal is not to pressure you into a new belief system but to liberate you from the pressure to fit into a faith community that draws its power from your learned smallness. By doing so, you will radically reshape your personal faith and expose the spaces in your life where real harm is being done. This is how deep and lasting healing happens.

Unlike many books and courses on faith deconstruction, the coming pages do not focus solely on healing the space(s) where you feel small or oppressed. In this book, you will begin by doing your own work first so that you can heal the generational, societal, and spiritual wounds that harm you and (falsely) give you permission to harm others.

Friend, I need to be really honest and tell you this is not a comfortable process, which is why not everyone chooses it. But it is an ancient, sacred experience that is well documented throughout church history. Even in the Bible, we see people working hard to untangle themselves from legalism, greed, and the fear of not being in control of everything and everyone. Many a sermon has been preached about the human fight against becoming hard-hearted. The problem is that legalism, nationalism, homophobia, transphobia, white saviorism, misogyny, and oppression of Black and Brown people are regularly presented as perfectly justified by scripture—often from the same pulpit.

The hypocrisy is frustrating, and it's driving people like you and me out of churches we never thought we'd leave. But we are not alone. People are leaving the church in record numbers, and this exodus shows no sign of slowing down any time soon. For many, deconstruction began (or at least accelerated) during the ramp-up to the 2016 American presidential election. Then-presidential candidate Donald Trump leveraged his bullying, gaslighting, and abusive self-promotion tactics to unite many evangelicals and fundamentalist Christians under his toxic banner.

As Trump's campaign gained momentum, it became clear that he was effectively garnering support from Christian voters by using garish sound bytes, calculated photo ops in Christian settings, and appeals to their fear of losing control of "their country." White Christians, particularly males, have always wielded more power in the broader church than any other group, but Trump invited them to adopt a narrative of victimhood—a false narrative where their anger was justified because their religion, families, and way of life were being attacked by their perceived enemies. The rhetoric focused on giving victimhood a place to fester, promising to retake Washington for conservative causes, and calling supporters to "Make America Great Again." They declared war and claimed it was a spiritual battle so that no tactics were off-limits.

Why was it so easy for evangelicals, fundamentalist Christians, and political conservatives to rally behind a candidate who clearly ignored Jesus's teachings about humility, loving neighbors, and providing for widows and the poor? Why could they support a candidate who thrived on the oppression of others?

The simple (yet extremely uncomfortable) answer is that all of these abusive tactics felt familiar and justified to many who've grown up in the American church. White Americans who didn't grow up in church but grew up in conservative, majority-Christian communities could easily find connections with Trump's tactics. In short, Trump's techniques worked because they were familiar. He followed the same playbook that religious leaders have been using to control their constituents for centuries. The approach felt familiar and resonated with what many white Christians had always heard in church, so they added their voices and resources to the political movement.

Then in early 2020, COVID-19 arrived and effectively poured tanker trucks full of gasoline onto the fire. Cries for racial justice in the summer of 2020 showed that Americans were at a point of reckoning with the harm we'd been doing to Black, Indigenous, and People of Color (BIPOC) for centuries. The "all lives matter" rhetoric became louder and more abusive, and evangelicals dug their heels in deep on hot-button issues and embraced their perceived victimhood.

Thankfully, not everyone absorbed the rhetoric and hate. Due mainly to the free flow of information on social media and unofficial news sources like blogs, another perspective rose to the surface. Experts began to call out the harm being done to marginalized people by the upswing in hateful rhetoric. People told their stories, shared research, and presented examples of how a country formed through the colonization and exploitation of others continued patterns of oppression.

Those of us who were listening to these stories learned about white privilege and fragility and started to understand how the American church was complicit in the genocide of America's Indigenous peoples and the enslavement of millions of men, women, and children. We heard historically accurate and meticulously researched reports of churches actively participating in the harmful practices while gaining money and power. We realized the narrative of the church as protector of marginalized people didn't hold water.

The COVID-19 shutdown also presented a unique opportunity for thousands of Christians who were quietly questioning their faith and feeling out of place in their faith communities. Suddenly, churches closed, and churchgoers had permission to stay home without having to excuse their absence. Many were surprised to feel relieved by not having to physically attend church. Even though the pandemic was scary and isolating, the release of pressure to put on a "church face" and remain silent about doubts was refreshing. There was now space to examine faith in new ways and without being surrounded by the echo chamber of an in-person faith community.

Christians turned to online communities to talk openly about doubts and how their faith was changing. Many discovered the term *faith deconstruction* and realized they'd been deconstructing for years without having a name for it. During the pandemic, discussion of deconstruction moved from private conversations with a few trusted friends into public conversations with strangers. Coaches and therapists who had been working in the faith deconstruction space for years found themselves inundated with new social media followers and clients asking for help.

Even though deconstruction has been around for centuries, it is gaining massive traction in the current season because of the horrific behavior of "good church people" in the last decade. Significant numbers of people are turning to faith deconstruction to help them find what is true, and Christians are just scratching the surface of answers because there are many who refuse to see deconstruction as a very normal, necessary stage of faith development.

Nearly everyone I've met in the deconstruction space longs for greater accountability and connection, not less. We aren't driven to deconstruct out of selfish motives or the desire to avoid being shaped and molded by our faith.

So, no—faith deconstruction isn't a trendy fad that's going to fade away as soon as something sexier comes along. When we choose to deconstruct our faith from toxic religion, we are choosing to challenge every single belief we hold and sit with uncomfortable truths about ourselves. This process is worth it for those who enter wholeheartedly and choose to relax their tightly clenched fists. There is liberating truth to be found in deconstruction and peace to be made with the mistakes of the past. Reconciling and releasing what does not move us closer to our Creator is what we are on this earth to do. You decide whether that means you identify as a Christian or not when it's all said and done.

Let's begin . . .

—

PART ONE

Understanding Where You Are

You probably didn't consciously choose to head into this season of deconstruction. Like most people who deconstruct their faith, you probably looked around one day and realized you weren't sure what you believed anymore. Now it feels like everything is unraveling and you don't have any say in what's happening to you or your faith. Nothing seems absolute and concrete. Everything you used to be sure of might seem questionable at best. You're likely feeling overwhelmed by questions like:

- Do I even want to be a Christian?
- Am I the only one struggling to figure out what I believe?
- What if I make the wrong choice about my faith?
- Am I going to lose it all?

I hope it puts your mind at ease to know your questions (and a whole bunch more) are totally normal and healthy. You're entering a season of deconstruction that is likely challenging everything you thought was unchallengeable about God and your faith, creating conflict in relationships you thought were rock solid, and leaving you exhausted. While this wilderness called deconstruction may feel overwhelming now, this is a sacred space for vulnerable exploration of everything you believe. It's a space for you to embrace curiosity, ask messy questions, and reconnect with yourself in ways you didn't know were possible.

Here, you don't have to match anyone else's definition of who you should be. You get to call the shots, take up as much space as you need, and set your own pace. In order to make that happen, you need to commit to showing up for yourself. You have to be your number one priority in this season. As you start sifting through all the information that's out there, you are going to have to learn to listen to and trust yourself. *You* are the best deconstruction guide for yourself, but that doesn't mean you have to do this alone. I'm here to give you my best tips, point you back to yourself, and offer encouragement to you on the hard days.

If you're feeling isolated, I hope it's helpful to know that you aren't the only one deconstructing and this isn't the first time there have been rumblings from within the Christian church. Historically, the church has gone through a major transformation every five hundred years. The birth of Christianity occurred two thousand years ago, followed by the fall of the Roman Empire five hundred years later and beginning the Dark Ages. In 1054, the Great Schism marked the separation of Eastern and Western Christian churches. The Reformation happened in the 1500s when the Protestant Church broke off from the Roman Catholic Church, and is one deconstruction many evangelicals discuss frequently.[1]

In her book *The Great Emergence*, the late Phyllis Tickle describes these massive shifts as "the 500-year rummage sale" to purge the church of what is no longer needed and make room for what is needed in the current season.[2] All the signs point to the current church being in the midst of another such shift. We—the church and anyone who has ever been part of it—are in a season I'm calling the Great Reckoning. Like during the Great Schism and the Reformation, present-day Christians are at a fork where the path diverges into two radically different directions.

Following one path requires doubling down on the imbalance of power and protecting the current church structure at all costs. The other path leads to a radical correction of the power imbalance by decentering white, patriarchal Christianity. Some Christians may say the shift is unnecessary or claim ignorance about the existence of the Great Reckoning. But those who are watching recognize we are rapidly approaching a tipping point where the current religious system will no longer have the support it needs to continue in its current form. This is primarily due to the connectedness of the world today and how quickly information flows from the source to audiences. However, it's also the result of many of us choosing the second path because we believe the religious abuse, genocide, and exploitation of people and resources cannot continue to go unnoticed.

The individual questioning and wrestling you're doing right now is the heart of the larger deconstruction movement. You're one of an increasingly large number of people who are crying out for revolution, reconciliation, and restitution in the church. Wherever you find yourself today, it's right where you're supposed to be. Even if everyone you know seems to be doubling down on the most harmful aspects of religion, it doesn't mean you're going the wrong way by choosing the other path. Others have the right to choose their path, just as you do.

It's time to give yourself the benefit of the doubt and permission to focus your attention on your next steps. This leg of your journey starts by busting a few myths about deconstruction, gaining a better understanding of what toxic religion is, confirming your hunch that toxic religion isn't an isolated issue in a handful of churches, and gathering some much-needed support for you to lean on during your deconstruction journey.

Yes, you're in the wilderness of deconstruction, but you are not alone. You have friends here. You've wandered into my camp and are welcome to warm yourself by my fire as long as you'd like. So pull up a camp chair, grab a s'more, and let's have a little chat about where you're headed next.

—

1

Explore the Heart of Deconstruction

I learned to be a people pleaser at an early age. We moved a lot, and I was always the new kid trying to figure out where I fit in. I learned how to read a room and assess who I needed to become to be accepted and liked. Usually, this meant being smart, funny, and willing to help people with anything they asked me to do. I knew my teachers liked me if I earned good grades and didn't make waves; I learned how to fall in line.

I tried to be perfect so that people would see me and accept me. I noticed that expressing certain emotions freaked people out, so I shoved those down and pretended I was okay.

Until I couldn't anymore.

I married young, had two children, and endured a nasty, drawn-out divorce before hitting rock bottom.

By the time I was in my mid-20s, I was highly experienced with rejection, bullying, and varying levels of abandonment. I was traumatized but didn't have a clue how to navigate it, so I just kept pretending and pushing. And then I had a breakdown. After months of running on empty, I attempted to take my own life before voluntarily checking into a mental hospital, only after being assured that the social worker could get an emergency court order to commit me if I didn't.

But I didn't stay long enough to get to the root of my pain. I was only there for a few days, detoxed from the random assortment of OTC meds I had taken, and checked myself out, determined to be better and stronger in the future. Instead of healing, I put on the old mask of someone who had her shit together. I just walled off all the hard, scary parts of my life and threw myself into nursing school in a new town where no one knew my story.

I relied on my old skills of reading the room and once more quickly figured out who I needed to become to be accepted by people around me. As long as I knew the rules and followed them, I would be safe and loved. I quickly made friends *and* made the dean's list. Hypervigilant, overachiever Angela was here to make up for all the bad decisions in her previous season of life, and she wasn't going away any time soon.

A few years later, when my new husband and I started going to church because "it would be good for our kids," I was ecstatic to find out that the rules and expectations there were pretty cut-and-dried. Following them didn't feel like legalism; the requirements felt like an instruction manual that laid out a plan for "how to be a better person" and, perhaps more important to me, "how to be accepted."

I embraced all facets of church life—first regularly attending Sunday service, then saying yes to an invitation to Sunday school, then beginning to volunteer during the week, and donating to special projects. I spent most of my free time listening to Christian music, reading Christian books, and watching Christian entertainment (of course, I knew all the best *Veggie Tales* songs).

After a few years of coloring inside the lines, it finally happened. For the first time in my life, I was totally "in." I was accepted. People with influence knew my name, and I knew all the inside jokes. I even enrolled in the local Christian university to pursue a degree in ministry.

At this point, you may be asking, "If it was all so good, how the heck did you end up *here*, up to your eyeballs in the deconstruction space?" The answer is simpler than you may think. Because my husband and I were "insiders," we were included in "insiders-only" conversations that rattled our belief that the church was the best place to raise our kids after all.

We were privy to conversations like the preschool leadership team debating whether an unmarried teacher should be removed because of her pregnancy; deciding on the exclusion of 2SLGBTQIA+[1] youth from the scouting troop; prioritizing a secondary kitchen space in the new addition over installing an elevator that would have made the shiny, new second-floor youth ministry area accessible to people with mobility issues; and discussing a sermon illustration where the punchline centered on the way a disabled man rode his bike. Y'all, there were literally *heated arguments* over whether or not the green carpet should be updated. I was there. I witnessed the worst of church pettiness—and church arrogance—all at once.

After all my years of fighting to fit in, I began to realize that maybe I didn't actually fit the mold. Maybe I didn't even like the mold at all. I began to wonder if I had more in common with the people being *excluded* from the community than the ones who were dictating the terms of belonging to it.

After many lengthy conversations, my husband and I assumed the bent toward conservative legalism was due to our church being 99.9 percent white, rural, and working/middle class. Eventually, we chose to move our family to a progressive, independent church in the center of town. Our new church was active in the surrounding neighborhood where we lived, operated a free after-school program for elementary-aged kids, and had a young, hipster, not-stuck-in-the-past vibe. Surely this would alleviate all of our concerns, right?

Sadly, after jumping into the leadership team and volunteering many hours there, I realized this new church was just as chaotic and just as harmful as our previous faith community. I will never forget sitting in the sanctuary following a choral performance by the children in the after-school program as teen volunteers from the church tried to motivate the congregation to support the ministry. They talked about the poverty and dysfunction of the families who utilized the program—while the children from that program sat next to them on stage and their "poverty-stricken, dysfunctional families," who had been invited as guests, sat in the audience. It was the most audacious and oblivious display of privilege and condescension I had ever witnessed.

I walked away with a pretty big case of #ChurchHurt and wondered how two radically different churches could be so harmful in such different, yet strangely similar ways.

I found myself in a season of wrestling with deep doubts. I was deconstructing from toxic religion, even though I didn't know that's what I was doing. I was just longing to get away from legalism because I'd realized not only did it not keep me safe, but it was doing real harm to others who can't fit themselves neatly into the white, conservative, church-box.

In hindsight, I now know this was the beginning of my deconstruction. My husband was mad at the people who had hurt us, and I was too, but I was also really, *really* mad at God for letting this happen on their watch.[2] After all, God called me to ministry. Why would they invite me into something and then not keep me safe?

I was so close to walking away from God and church, yet still fighting hard to find a faith community that I could trust.

Developing a Shared Language

Before we talk about navigating deconstruction, it's essential to define what deconstruction is and what it isn't. Like the many expressions of faith that are in existence, people have a lot of different meanings for deconstruction, and it can create confusion if we are using different definitions.

In this section, I'll introduce you to a handful of terms and phrases we will use throughout our time together. The goal is to create some shared language around deconstruction so that we can more easily navigate its complexities. I am fully aware that every term and phrase is nuanced. The term *deconstruction* will have slightly different meanings for each person depending on the reader's context. If you're reading this book, it is likely you are moving away from a toxic religious environment where leaders insisted on certain interpretations of terms. Unlike those leaders, I will not insist that the way I define these words is the only interpretation or even the most correct based on the origin of the root word. Instead, I present these definitions as the meaning we will use *in this setting* so that we can better understand faith deconstruction, toxic religion, and each other.

Deconstruction is a term for a philosophical and literary theory stemming from the mid-twentieth century work of Jacques Derrida. Derrida described deconstruction as a way of moving past the limited perspective of concrete answers and absolutism. He stated that the majority of ideas philosophers pondered, like truth and justice, were significantly more complex than we believed. Trying to reduce complex ideas to simple black and white concepts leads to a lack of understanding on our part.

Instead, Derrida argued that to truly understand complex ideas, we need to allow space for the gray areas and nuanced meanings. Those gray areas and nuances stand in direct opposition to the legalism and absolutism of toxic religion. Giving yourself permission to be uncertain and to explore allows you to move through deconstruction more smoothly. Deconstruction is rarely easy, but it is significantly harder when we insist on our need to have exact answers.

Derrida also warned that deconstruction is not a formulaic process that can be dictated from one person to another. A rigid, cookie-cutter process with a specific end in mind may shift some beliefs you learned in toxic religious environments, but it won't release you from the root cause of those harmful stances.

You may be scratching your head and asking how I am going to help you deconstruct if this book won't give you the exact steps to do so. The good news is that in my ten-plus years as a coach, I've noticed the patterns in deconstruction work, seen where people get stuck, and have gathered hundreds of resources to help you navigate the hardest parts of your deconstruction journey without stirring up shame, scarcity, or pressure to fit in. Remember, the goal is to be curious and vulnerable while exploring faith with open hands. You don't have to measure up to anyone's expectations or try to deconstruct exactly like someone else did. This is *your* sandbox to play in and *you* get to call the shots.

As you read this book, you'll discover new tools, processes, and activities that will help you embrace the gray. What you're about to learn is your very own Choose Your Own Adventure guide to deconstruction. The words are already on the pages, but you get to choose what feels most resonant, and your destination has yet to be determined. Think of this book as a guide that supportively walks beside you as you explore instead of as the unrelenting voice of a direction app that anticipates where you are and barks out your next step to get to the destination it's programmed to send you.

Religious deconstruction is based on Derrida's philosophical foundation. For some, it takes a slightly different tack because, after faith deconstruction, there are usually still certain absolute beliefs and structures that remain, which was not the case in Derrida's original vision for the term. In faith deconstruction, we are not dismantling every belief we have until there is no belief left. Instead, we are examining, sifting, and sorting what we believe to determine how it aligns with who we believe God to be.

Most of us start with two buckets. The first bucket holds the parts of our faith that are worth salvaging, and in the second bucket, we place the things we no longer believe should be in our belief system. While that sounds relatively simple, I have to caution you that it isn't. We must heed Derrida's warning against a formulaic process. Within every single bucket, there is a range of possibilities. Instead of only two buckets, there is an infinite number of buckets, and they are all only slightly different from each other. For example, we will likely identify beliefs that we really want to rescue from toxic religion but are unsure if they can be separated from the misogynistic, patriarchal roots that taught us to believe them in the first place.

Faith deconstruction does not always lead to deconversion. In this experience, you are not being asked to throw away everything you believe and completely walk away from God. Sometimes that happens, but contrary to what deconstruction's critics say, it isn't the goal. Instead, the goal for most who deconstruct is to strip away all of the false doctrines that have been used to justify patriarchy, racism, white supremacy, misogyny, homophobia, transphobia, and forced conversion to Christianity. Deconstruction isn't abandoning one's faith; it's abandoning the abusive belief system that we were conditioned to believe was God's will. At its core, faith deconstruction moves us closer to what a vibrant spiritual life was always supposed to be.

We are deconstructing from toxic religion with the hopes of rooting out the beliefs that harm us and (falsely) give us God's permission (or even an obligation) to harm others. This experience requires us to unlearn the legalism and fragility we picked up from Bible translations manipulated by the people who funded their creation.

Defining *Toxic Religion*

One phrase you'll hear me use over and over is *toxic religion*. This phrase refers to unhealthy doctrines, legalism, and abusive practices that are deeply connected to Christianity and the church. Not all toxic beliefs or harmful behaviors are connected to religion or Christianity specifically.

In this book, what qualifies as toxic religion is when God, the Bible, the church, or faith in general are used to justify problematic behavior. For example, when Bible verses are quoted out of context to "prove" that God backs an oppressive idea or behavior and this idea or behavior becomes the cultural norm in the faith community. That norm may spread outside of the church community to places like schools, workplaces, and governments when Christians enter those spaces and impose their beliefs on others.

One of the harmful hallmarks of toxic religion is a total lack of self-awareness on the part of Christians. Instead of being curious and open to consider messy questions, Christians embedded in toxic religion are taught to shut down such conversations by firing off quippy responses. It would be considered totally normal to double down on an unexamined position by saying things like "The Bible clearly says," or "Love the sinner, hate the sin," or "I'll pray for you."

I know hearing the above definition will create some discomfort. If you, like me, have been inside the church for very long, there's a good chance you've embraced toxic religion too. I feel myself squirming a little writing this because I know I have imposed my beliefs on others in the past. We will spend more time reflecting on this later, but for now, just know that this is a space where you'll learn to navigate both the harm that's been done to you and the harm you've done in toxic religious spaces.

Unplugging from the Matrix

In the 1999 mind-bending sci-fi hit *The Matrix*, the hero Neo becomes aware that two realities exist. Neo's daily life was actually an illusion created by a powerful and abusive race of sentient beings. After defeating humanity in a catastrophic war, these beings developed a system of siphoning human life force to power their civilization. With the help of a handful of other humans who are also aware of the illusion, Neo learns that to maintain the power source, the sentient beings created the Matrix, which presents an illusion of a meaningful, connected, and relatively safe life. Neo's real life that exists outside the Matrix is much harsher than the civilized and mundane life he thought was real. In the postapocalyptic world, several groups of rebels try to release people and defeat the Matrix (as prophesied by the Oracle).

Although we now know the Wachowski sisters created the movie franchise as a metaphor for being transgender, when *The Matrix* released, all that was clear was that they were calling attention to the harm done by oppressive systems.[3] At the heart of Neo's story is an awakening to the toxic abusive system that siphons power from those who are plugged into it. Choice is present for those connected to the Matrix, but only within the allowed parameters. Neo quickly discovers that getting curious and asking the wrong questions provokes the wrath of Agents, who are the defenders of the Matrix.

Thankfully, we humans have never been used as batteries for another species, but toxic religion is an abusive system that drains power from those who are part of it. Whether that power takes the form of money, social standing, or political influence, it is always funneled away from the most marginalized people groups and leveraged to benefit the powerful. Toxic religion's Matrix is the Christian bubble where the illusion of autonomy, acceptance, and deep connection with the Divine exists. Life within the bubble is pleasant as long as we are willing to assimilate into the existing structure without angering the religious gatekeepers (Agents).

Deconstruction isn't only about examining our own lives and the impact toxic religion has on us. It also invites us into a complex conversation about how our actions and beliefs uphold the toxic system because in some ways, we benefit from this system. Embedding ourselves in a toxic religious community provides connection, acceptance, and a certain level of protection from the harsher aspects of life. Like Neo's awakening, deconstruction invites us to unplug from the Matrix's illusion and step outside the perceived safety of our current belief system. The real world, which sometimes feels just as brutal as the Matrix's postapocalyptic Zion, is a space filled with unknowns.

It's easy to challenge doctrines and cultural mandates that harm us without ever learning about and reconciling the harm we are doing to others. This is a common problem Christians run into in this jolting world of uncertainty. Deconstructing one aspect of toxic religion should create a chain reaction of questioning and challenging every other aspect of our belief system. But, because of our conditioning to defer to the existing power structure, to stay connected to the Matrix and not relinquish our position in the hierarchy, the chain reaction often doesn't happen.

For example, it's common for white, middle-class Christian women to feel the sting of gender bias that keeps them out of the pulpit, pays them significantly less per hour than their male counterparts, and pressures them to take on hundreds of hours per month of unpaid labor to manage their household (labor that isn't shared by their partner). In search of guidance, these women begin reading about the passages that have been used to perpetuate this bias in Christian circles. Perhaps the women discover the way the meaning of key words in 1 Timothy 2:12 and 1 Corinthians 14:34–35 were translated to reflect the culture's preference for devaluing women.

As a result, instead of seeing the "equal but different" arguments (also called *complementarianism*) as God's will, the women's beliefs on this topic change. With no safe place to express these new beliefs, that's usually where this particular exploration stops. It doesn't extend to asking, If those passages had been twisted to devalue everything feminine, what other passages have been similarly twisted and who else has been negatively impacted? We rarely ask who we are harming by benefiting from these twisted translations, but we must if we really want to deconstruct from toxic religion. Our desire to be free from our own oppression isn't the same as changing our entire belief system around gender bias. One belief has been changed, but not the entire set of beliefs related to this topic.

Deconstruction is a radical change to our belief system, which means that we have to go beyond trying to release ourselves from bad doctrines that harm us to also releasing ourselves from the bad doctrines from which we benefit.

In this example about the equality of women, that means looking at the way Christianity's devaluation of all things feminine feeds the bad doctrines of homophobia, transphobia, misogyny, and toxic masculinity. As a white, heterosexual/cisgender woman (meaning I am non-2SLGBTQIA+ and my gender identity matches the one I was assigned at birth), I may be harmed by gender bias, but I am not harmed to the same extent as queer and trans women who are regularly called "unnatural" and "an abomination" by the church and who have limited rights and protection from the American government.

So in this example, deconstructing requires us to do our own work around gender bias and recognize that the marginalization of trans women is one hundred percent rooted in the same bad translations that present women under male authority as God's original plan. Cisgender women must push beyond our own limited perspective and listen to how those who live in the intersection of being trans and a woman are deeply harmed by the internalized misogyny we express on a daily basis.

If my deconstruction only frees *me* from oppressive doctrines, it's not actually deconstruction; it's self-preservation.

Seem confusing? Think of it this way: In Mark 5:43–47, Jesus says that we should not only love our neighbors but also love our enemies. It's easy and completely logical to love people who are kind to us, but it's more challenging and more revolutionary to care for people who do not love us. In the same way, Christians are called to dismantle systems we benefit from at the expense of others. For example, women are likely to stand against misogyny because it obviously harms women. When men work to dismantle their own misogynistic beliefs and undercut the systems that unfairly favor them, they're engaging in true deconstruction.

I want to be very clear that I'm not reinforcing the white savior paradigm where those of us who are white go out and attempt to "save" people of color who are "lesser" because of their standing in the patriarchal hierarchy. White saviorism upholds toxic religion and continues to shift power from the marginalized to the top of the food chain.

I implore you to reject the "us versus them" narrative when it comes to thinking about white people or people of color. Othering *always* supports the existing oppressive systems. Deconstruction requires a "we" narrative: one where we leverage the resources and benefits available to us so that we can radically shift our belief systems and flatten the patriarchal hierarchy.

Simply swapping out one doctrine for another isn't faith deconstruction. It's just switching sides on a hot-button issue. External pressure creates change, so when political and social movements gain momentum, there can be external pressure to change your beliefs on the topics that concern the people around you. External pressure may convince you that something feels off, and your logical brain starts examining data. You may take in more and more info and realize you've been doing something wrong or missing a valuable perspective. You can commit to doing things differently, and your behavior relating to that topic begins to change. You've changed a belief, and you might be able to say you deconstructed your beliefs around *that specific topic*.

But deconstructing your belief system comes from an internal pressure and starts with an internal shift. There is likely still a precipitating event—a catalyst that leads you to say that something is not right—but unlike deconstructing around a single topic, this is a systemic deconstruction. You may question your identity, your faith, and the role you play in an unjust system. You consume more information and recognize how your identity has been shaped by false beliefs and unhealthy doctrines. You change how you carry yourself and how you participate in the system that you benefited from previously. You commit to doing things differently, and your behavior begins to change, even without the certainty of knowing you are "right."

Being right is the goal of someone trying to preserve or advance their place in the Christian hierarchy, but deconstruction is a complete rewiring of our identity so that we are no longer plugged into that hierarchy at all. The old toxic religious belief system is like the Matrix; it can't define our values or dictate our actions if we unplug from it.

Letting Go of Granny's Biscuit Recipe

I learned really early how to insert myself into the narrative around me. I was a color-outside-of-the-lines kid at heart, but being who I was expected to be and following the rules was what allowed me to fit in. I tell you this to let you know that I completely understand your desire to have a deconstruction checklist that tells you exactly what steps you can take to untangle from toxic religion. It would make it so much easier if you knew what was expected of you and how to make it happen.

Unfortunately, I can't do that because I want *you* to deconstruct, not just shift from what you used to believe to what *I* think you should believe. The truth is, giving you a deconstruction checklist would only reinforce the patterns of toxic religion. It would invite you to see me as a guru or mentor to lead you on a set path toward truth. But following what I say is not deconstruction; it is just shifting from one unhealthy belief system to another that's slightly less toxic. It's switching sides in an argument without actually getting to the root cause of the toxicity and forming your own understanding.

Your deconstruction journey will likely challenge the way you were taught to take in and evaluate information. If you were raised in a logical, authoritarian, or legalistic upbringing (like most American evangelical settings) deconstruction is going to ask you to turn down the voices demanding certainty and embrace curiosity instead. The work of deconstruction happens in gray areas, and there will often be more than one right answer to the questions raised by the process.

Instead of steps on a linear pathway, your deconstruction will look more like a Venn diagram with constantly shifting circles. Every time you challenge a piece of your belief system, the circles will adjust to meet you where you are. At times, fluidity can be unbelievably frustrating for people who are used to following instructions and falling in line, but it's what is needed to set you free from toxic religion.

Faith deconstruction is a healing experience that must be individualized based on your need. It's not your granny's tried-and-true biscuit recipe (the one that's been made a million times and always produces perfectly flakey morsels). Each person needs different information, conversations, and supportive environments (think of unique ingredients and equipment) to successfully deconstruct from toxic religion because we all reached this breaking point in different ways.

Instead of Granny's biscuit recipe, think of deconstruction like an ice cream sundae bar loaded with a dozen flavors, toppings, and sauces. You get to decide if a sugar cone or a waffle bowl is what you need to feel supported in this season. Maybe you don't even want ice cream right now, so instead, you fill a bowl with hot fudge, glop on whipped cream, and stick a straw in your concoction.

The goal is to gather ingredients and develop practices to help you deconstruct bad doctrines, understand the privilege you have in a white Christian patriarchal hierarchy, and recognize your ability to choose a different path. Don't get me wrong, I love a good biscuit—I mean, *checklist*—but that can't be the only thing in your life.

Predictability and making you toe the line to fit in is a big part of the way toxic religion has taught you to shrink. Why? Because predictability and your fear of not fitting in with your faith community make you easier to control and uphold the power imbalance. (We will spend more time on this topic in chapter 2; for now, just know that you feel the need to fit in because toxic religious leaders groomed you to feel that way.)

Going with the Flow

You may not believe me yet, but I promise that the flowing circle model of faith deconstruction will actually serve you better than the rigid linear process you may be longing for right now. Why? Because toxic religion and other oppressive systems thrive when followers see the world in absolutes. A great example of this is the "us versus them" mindset that creates so much division in communities.[4]

Consider where you get your news and how you spend your free time. Are you surrounded by gaslighting, defensiveness, and bullying? I advise you to take a step back from all the screamers, even the ones you agree with, while you work through this book. Why? Because deconstructing is hard on your body, and there comes a point where people who are constantly pushing your nervous system into the fight, flight, freeze, or fawn mode are not helpful. While they may have been the catalyst for your deconstruction and helped you tap into the rage that was buried deep, it's possible to be grateful and also step away in this season.

I highly recommend loosening your grip on certainty and embracing the gray areas of life. Get used to not having all the answers, and learn to sit with your fear of being abandoned if you don't fit in. Shadow work, or diving into the complex or repressed parts of ourselves, requires a release of tight-fisted emotional control. By embracing openhandedness and letting your tender parts show, you give yourself permission to stop fighting to fit in. You'll finally have the resources and desire to shift away from the toxic beliefs that made you feel safe before you realized how harmful they were.

This is where the magic happens and lasting transformations occur. Big feelings have deep roots, so be kind and patient with yourself. It's so very important not to expect this to happen overnight.

Dealing with Reconstruction

Reconstruction of your faith is not a given on a deconstruction journey because what you need is determined by where you are and how you got there. Each person's journey is unique, but in my work with clients I've identified three common situations that deconstructors find themselves in. In some cases, the only way to get away from toxic religion is to jump in the car, drive it off a cliff Thelma-and-Louise style, and figure out your next steps after you land. I see this occur when people are so deeply embedded in toxic religion that the pain is threatening their physical survival. Sometimes what you need to do is walk (or run) from everything you used to consider as Truth without looking back.

Burning it all down and walking away is a second method of deconstruction that's a little more like demolition. You're left with a big pile of beliefs and experiences to sift through and decide if anything is worth keeping. In this case, and if you want to have any beliefs about faith in your post-deconstruction life, you'll likely need to spend some time reconstructing. If this is the way you get away from toxic religion—*high five!* Go for it! Remember, deconstruction is fluid and can always bend to meet you where you are.

There's also a third model of deconstruction that allows room for sifting and sorting beliefs in real time. This model is less about demolishing beliefs and more like disassembling a complex machine and looking for pieces that shouldn't be there. And it's a bit like applying Marie Kondo's method of tidying up a home to your belief system. The answer to one question determines whether or not her clients keep each household item being sorted. Instead of asking if each belief sparks joy, à la Marie Kondo, you'll ask if each belief honors who you know God to be.

- Do your beliefs about 2SLGBTQIA+ people reflect a Creator who fashioned all people in their image?
- Does aligning with a legalistic, patriarchal evangelical church represent a Divine being who cherishes the spunky creativity and free spirit you were born with?
- Does pursuing constant hustle and "fake it till you make it" capitalism honor a God who wired humans for rest, play, and connection?

Because you're reading this book, I'm going to assume that you're already asking these questions. You're probably feeling the tension of knowing that honest answers will change everything. Perhaps you're vacillating between being terrified of losing your faith and being so pissed that you'd rather walk away than spend one more day in a community that's doing so much harm. Your family and church friends may be completely avoiding you or pressuring you to stop rocking the boat. You may feel totally worn out already.

Trying to manage all those things and the emotions they're bringing up is exhausting. If you're wondering if your faith is even worth saving, you're in the perfect place to dive into deconstruction . . . because, at its core, deconstruction isn't about fixing your faith, or fitting in at your church, or fully understanding what the Bible says. Instead, turn your attention toward getting out from under the weight of the toxic religious teachings that are smothering you.

This is the season for learning how to have your own back, nurturing your own tender spaces, and trusting yourself enough to explore this wilderness called deconstruction.

There's time and space right here and right now for you to do this—on your own terms.

2

Beware the Wolf in Deconstructionist Clothing

Faith deconstruction isn't about saving the church or tearing it down. It's not actually about the church at all—it's about people finding a way to cling to God despite the harm the church has done to them and the harm they've done while part of the church. It's a personal faith experience where the goal is to break down our beliefs into smaller pieces, challenge them, and see what holds up.

Some critics say that deconstruction is the easy way out for selfish people who don't want to see the church change and heal. The church is certainly due for a reformation from the inside, where powerful people hold other powerful people accountable for the harm they're doing in God's name. Perhaps more people deconstructing will even lead to that type of reformation. But that's not what deconstruction is. Deconstruction is a personal journey that moves one toward a healthy, mature faith and away from toxic religious teachings.

The Goal of Deconstruction

The best part of deconstruction is getting to strip away all of toxic religion's false doctrines and look around to see what's Divine. If you or the people in your support system are prioritizing the survival of existing church systems, then the healing you need isn't driving the deconstruction process and it's unlikely you'll find the peace you are craving.

Church leaders find faith deconstruction scary because many of the false doctrines and abusive practices that uphold the imbalanced power structures of the white evangelical church don't withstand scrutiny. Deconstruction is a threat to toxic religion. In the imbalanced power structure of a church deeply rooted in systems of oppression like white supremacy, anyone who has power stands to lose a little of that power if other members deconstruct. Those who have been marginalized by toxic religion stand to gain significant power and influence by disengaging from the systems that pushed them to the margin in the first place.

It is nearly impossible to dismantle toxic systems from within by putting the survival of that system first. For the insiders who truly love the church and thrive in the current imbalanced power structure, deconstruction certainly threatens life as they know it, but what most don't see is that deconstruction is likely the spark for reformation that will eventually bring massive healing to the church.

The need for healing is real. There are too many stories to write this off as a couple of unhealthy churches operating under bad leadership. I hear stories of #ChurchHurt all the time in my job as a faith deconstruction coach. Although everyone's experience is unique, patterns emerge. I want to take a few moments to share some client-approved snippets because I have a hunch you'll see your own story in the words of a few of my clients.[1]

- I met Joanna, a single woman in her twenties when she reached out to me for faith deconstruction coaching. She believed in God, felt that regular church attendance was important for faith development, and loved praying and reading her Bible. However, she was struggling to reconcile her sexuality with her conservative upbringing. She was keenly aware that the mostly elderly, evangelical church community she grew up in would not welcome her as a gay woman. So, she stopped going.

She knew without a doubt that she was gay. What she didn't know was if God was okay with that. Joanna had already lost her parents, grandmother, and the church community she grew up in; thinking about losing God terrified her. She worried that God would consider her desire for a wife sinful. She loved God desperately, even when "good church people" had hurt her, and couldn't bear to think about God pushing her away.

- When I met Yolanda, she was struggling to find her place in the church where she used to feel so welcomed. Her marriage was falling apart, she was questioning her sexuality, and she was feeling really confused about how those changes might impact her relationship with God. Her faith community kept telling her to try harder and to be a better wife. Yolanda was told that her lack of faith was the source of her doubts and stress.

  Yolanda was stuck and couldn't decide what she wanted or needed because she was terrified of losing every relationship she cared about. Yolanda told me, "I was going through the motions of what I was taught was pleasing to God, but it didn't feel right and gave me anxiety. I had a lot of questions but was afraid to ask them, and didn't know who or where to ask them."

- Gemma sought out coaching during faith deconstruction because she was overwhelmed by the shame she felt about being uncertain in her faith. She had spent a few years in the evangelical church before spending the next decade in a fundamentalist group. She saw a lot of harm being done by the church, which claimed to represent God, but she also had deep moments of feeling personally connected to God. She went from being an active leader in her faith community to not even attending weekly service. She began to worry that people were being harmed because she encouraged them to join her unhealthy faith community.

  Gemma stopped trusting herself and began to rely on everyone else's opinion of who she should be and what she should believe. The COVID-19 pandemic provided much-needed separation from her church, and she realized she felt calmer, healthier, and safer when she didn't attend. Not having to "fake it" every week gave her the space she needed to get honest about how little she believed anymore.

- Sally was a firecracker of an overachiever who excelled in a church leadership role until her faith began to crumble. She was shocked when the anti-2SLGBTQIA+ rhetoric explode during the 2016 presidential election. She saw real people she loved being hurt. Her personal connection to the targets of hate made her question her "Love the sinner, hate the sin" stance. Seeing multiple social media posts and articles about the prevalence of homophobia in the church prompted Sally to wonder if she had it all wrong. She wondered if her stance, which had seemed perfectly clear and backed by the Bible, was wrong, what else could she be getting wrong?

  Her questions were not well received by her church community, and she was pushed out of her ministry leadership role. Angry, brokenhearted, and still wanting to do what was right, Sally threw her hands up and walked away from the church. Even in her frustration, there was a small voice in the back of her mind that kept saying, "But what if God is real?" She chose to privately wrestle with her uncertainty.

Perhaps you felt a hint of recognition while reading those stories. If not, that's okay. Your faith deconstruction story is just as valid, and you are welcome here. *Everyone* is welcome here. It's crucial to underscore that even if your entire church community has rejected you because of your questions and doubts, you are not alone.

The Isolation of Deconstruction

One of the biggest reasons Christians don't deconstruct from toxic religion is because we've been conditioned to believe that being part of the faith community we were raised in is crucial to maintain our spiritual, mental, emotional, and physical health. When we begin to deconstruct, our doubts and questions can make people feel very uncomfortable, and our acceptance in the faith community we love is often threatened.

Often when someone starts asking questions that fall out of bounds with their faith community, there's an instant urge to "offer counsel and correction" before the questioner goes "too far." Those who raise questions that are "too much" or challenge the current imbalanced power structure receive heavy-handed criticism about their intelligence, ethics, and general understanding of God, the church, and Christianity. Questioners are often warned that they are caving to societal pressures, lacking in discipline to follow God's will, or are embracing sin because they want to be rebellious.

In many cases, these responses come from people who are sincerely worried about the faith deconstruction journeys of friends and family. The concern arises because they want to keep people from adopting harmful beliefs, which isn't a bad thing. Where that concern jumps the shark is when Christians leverage shame, loss of community, and gaslighting tactics to scare people away from exploring complex aspects of their faith. People who are expressing genuine concern about the possibility of others losing faith don't frustrate deconstructors with their concern—it's their lack of curiosity and determination to preserve the person's faith as it stands at any cost.

It's very common for those who speak up to be shamed back into submission, or at least into silence about their doubts in order to quiet the criticism from people who claim to be speaking on God's behalf. Shunning, ex-communication, and shaming are often used to discourage faith deconstruction because they work, especially when doled out by people in someone's innermost circle.

Toxic religion controls people with tactics designed to tap into deep feelings of wanting to be accepted in order to activate inner fear of abandonment. These tactics are abusive and manipulative.

The prevalence of these tactics in the church is a big reason powerful leaders can get away with tremendous amounts of abuse without being confronted or challenged by those who know what's going on.

The Backlash against Deconstruction

In the summer of 2021, *The Rise and Fall of Mars Hill* podcast, published by *Christianity Today*, went viral. It told the story of Mark Driscoll's shift from being the evangelical super pastor to the poster child for abusive Christian leaders. Pastors, church leaders, and evangelical authors shared their perspectives on the podcast via social media and blogs. They expressed grief about the effects of Driscoll's behavior, debated the causes, and created step-by-step plans to keep other organizations from going down the same road. Each new episode generated more opinions, predictions, and Aesop's-fable-like lessons we should learn from Mars Hill's failure. The story was shocking to hear for many, and people could not ignore it.

However, not everyone was shocked by the overwhelming toxicity of Mark Driscoll, the Mars Hill leadership team, and the overarching culture of the Mars Hill community.[2] Many of us listeners had experienced firsthand harm in toxic and abusive religious communities, so the revelations on the podcast were unsurprising. The fallout from the podcast was similar to when the official reports came to light about famed apologist Ravi Zacharias harassing, abusing, and trafficking women.[3] The comparison was clear: the organization that surrounded Mark Driscoll prioritized his power and legacy over the protection of vulnerable congregants. This specific kind of traumatic experience, commonly called "church hurt," led some Christians to walk away from faith altogether, while others (like me) chose deconstruction.

As I write this in the spring of 2022, there's a severe up-tick of articles, podcasts, and social media content published by people within the church trying to explain deconstruction. A quick internet search for "faith deconstruction" will yield results from behemoth Christian organizations like *The Gospel Coalition*, *Christianity Today*, and *Relevant* magazine. Individuals like Carey Nieuwhof, Tish Harrison Warren, Matt Chandler, and Alisa Childers created widely circulated content warning about the dangers of deconstruction and advising pastors to keep their congregation safe from this "trendy movement." In front of thousands of teens at a Winter Jam concert, Christian rocker John Cooper shouted, "It is time that we declare war against this deconstruction Christian movement. I don't even like calling it deconstruction Christian. There is nothing Christian about it. It is a false religion."[4]

I used the word *explain* loosely above because insiders write the majority of this content for other insiders who are just trying to mitigate the fallout from something they see as a threat to the system in which they're thriving. Rarely do they include input from people who have deconstructed. It's very much akin to the fox guarding the henhouse and telling the hens that there's tremendous danger outside the walls that supposedly protect them.

Perhaps even more dangerous are those leaders who quote Christians who've chosen to deconstruct one aspect of toxic religion that impacted them but still openly harm others by holding on to unhealthy religious beliefs. For example, a few high-profile hetero/cis women have spoken out against gender bias against women without calling out the unbiblical homophobia rooted in the same devaluation of all things feminine. Another example is those leaders who openly support social justice causes in war-torn countries but deny the need for Christians to come to terms with and make reparations for the ongoing genocide of North America's Indigenous people.

Leaders who have worked on deconstructing a single topic are often touted as experts who dabbled in deconstruction and got close to that slippery slope but heroically returned to the core teachings of primarily white evangelical churches.

It seems problematic, doesn't it?

Well, that's because it is.

If you want to understand what faith deconstruction is, why so many people are drawn to it, and what the results are, you'd be better served talking to people who've fully deconstructed instead of those who are threatened by the idea and are lashing out without further exploration.

The Church's Response to Deconstruction

One thing that history proves over and over again is that if there's anything that threatens the imbalanced power structure of the church, she has a few common ways of protecting herself. Here are a few of the tactics being used by those who want to preserve the existing structure.

Discrediting and Dismissing

I'm sure you've encountered examples of anti-deconstruction articles, blogs, podcasts, sermons, and YouTube videos. The goal of these resources is for Christian leaders to "get ahead" of the deconstruction curve and convince people that it's a sinful, selfish process that basically boils down to rebellion against God. If the church can convince us to avoid questioning and challenging the status quo, then the status quo of imbalanced power structure remains intact. This tactic to discredit and dismiss deconstruction, which usually includes a lot of contempt, belittling, and defensiveness, is heavily favored by theologically fundamentalist and conservative churches because they regularly rely on fear of hell, consequences to sin, and God's wrath to steer people away from questioning.

Co-opting and Redefining the Term

This tactic is often deployed by churches with moderate to more progressive theologies. It involves reducing the threat that deconstruction poses by watering it down to reflect the church's progressive theology and repackaging it into sermon series and small groups. The risk here is that instead of dismantling the entirety of toxic religion, these organizations are focused on taking down specific doctrines they don't agree with and misnaming that process deconstruction. They may even self-examine to root out subtle remnants of white supremacy or anti-2SLGBTQIA+ sentiments, which makes the church healthier but still encourages assimilation into their version of Christianity.

The goal is often presented as deconstructing without losing our faith, but as we've already discussed, true deconstruction doesn't allow us to dictate where we will land. Insisting that faith remains intact takes some questions off the table and restricts our ability to follow deconstruction wherever it leads.

Pushing for Systemic Reformation (Not Deconstruction)

This tactic is already being deployed by highly visible evangelical bloggers and pastors. The goal is to shift a person's focus away from individual deconstruction and point them toward creating systemic change within the church instead. Most people who are deconstructing would agree that the church needs a massive overhaul, so this idea can be an easy sell. But again, focusing on systemic reformation instead of deconstruction is rooted in an attempt to keep people inside the current religious system. Pressure is applied to "be the change" instead of "selfishly" leaving the church and doing your own deconstruction thing.

Insisting that people focus on overhauling the system that is harming them *right now* reflects one of the most traumatic pillars of abuse. It puts the burden of the responsibility for fixing a broken system on those who are being oppressed by that system rather than stacking the majority of the responsibility on those who benefit from the oppression of others. People who are being pushed out of the church by toxic religion are not responsible for fixing her from the inside. That responsibility lies squarely on the shoulders of those holding an inordinate amount of power.

Calling for reformation instead of deconstruction also completely misses the point: reformation takes decades, if not centuries, to create large-scale change. You cannot change a system from within its walls unless you're willing to relinquish the benefits you receive from the imbalance of power. Personal deconstruction is required to create broader reformation. Both individual and systemic changes are needed.

Twisting Reconstruction into Evangelism

While you are deconstructing, it is important to look out for signs that those offering to help you might actually try to keep you engaged with the unhealthy system from which you're trying to break free. Reconstruction might occur at the end of your deconstruction journey, but it also might not. Be alert to those who emphasize the importance of faith reconstruction over the necessity of faith deconstruction first. They will likely encourage you to preserve the core of your belief system at all costs and continue to lean on your religious community for support. While this may sound like solid advice, it can lead to additional trauma for those who are embedded in toxic communities.

People who use this tactic seek to re-engage people who've walked away from the church. They present deconstruction as a trendy name for rebellion or deconversion, and they present reconstruction (led by religious leaders, of course) as the next logical step. A few highly visible Christian influencers are lifted up as examples of people who experienced seasons of doubt, and perhaps even dabbled in deconstruction, but came back to their senses and back into the fold.[5] The plethora of books, articles, and podcasts attempting to leverage deconstruction as an evangelistic tool is evidence of this tactic's deployment by religious leaders.

CHAPTER 2

The Bottom Line for Deconstruction

Moving away from white supremacy, legalism, and bad doctrines certainly seems like something that would move people toward a healthier faith, so why isn't the church embracing deconstruction? The simple answer is that unhealthy systems are threatened by people getting healthy.

What most critics of deconstruction don't realize is that their angry, dismissive, and bullying responses simply confirm the need to challenge what's acceptable within the church.

The pushback against deconstruction is spearheaded by those who haven't deconstructed and have a significant influence on the current power structure. Apologists and talking heads who have been trained to defend the gospel with intellect and power-plays have "declared war" on deconstruction with a cult-like fervor that is typically reserved for the most "threatening" social movements like abolition and desegregation.

When the most powerful people and organizations are on the offensive against a movement, it should cause us to take a step back and ask who has the most to gain if the movement dies out. It's certainly not God or the people on the margins that the church is supposed to be caring for—and *that's why we need deconstruction.*

So no, we will not put away this spiritual awakening we call deconstruction. It is a sacred, holy movement toward an equitable community of people exploring faith. Here, in the wilderness of deconstruction, there is room to follow Jesus if you want to, without defensively abusing, belittling, and dehumanizing those who don't.

—

Criticism and pushback are why many Christians stay silent about their doubts, and in turn their faith gets smaller and smaller. Many deconstructing Christians decided not to return to church immediately after COVID-19 restrictions were lifted; they found themselves feeling happier, calmer, and safer without regular church attendance. Here we return to the stories from my clients.

- Joanna wasn't ready to give up on her faith. She worked hard to challenge the flawed theology and manipulated Bible translations that led her old church to preach anti-2SLGBTQIA+ doctrines. She gradually came out to her brother, a couple of old friends she trusted, and eventually to her followers on social media. Her courage was rewarded with love and acceptance, which she knows is not always the case for Christians like her. "I'm good with God. I know He loves me, created me as a lesbian, and adores who I am," Joanna says. But trusting a church community has been harder. For this season, Joanna feels safe to attend an accepting (but non-affirming) online church, but she also knows this is not a permanent home. She longs to find a church home and community that welcomes her whole identity.
- Yolanda separated from her husband, took a step back from church participation, and began attending therapy several times per week to explore the source of her pain. She later shared with me how unhealthy relationships had completely swallowed her to the point she was filled with self-loathing. The effects of purity culture, aggressive sermons about hell, and constantly fearing she was a disappointment to God completely depleted the confidence she had as a child.
- Gemma is still peeling back layers of old beliefs and examining each one, but she has finally released herself from the pressure to be absolutely certain all the time. As she loosened her grip on perfection and certainty, she found the courage to trust herself again. "I may not yet know exactly what I believe," she says. "But I am confident I am the only one who has permission to tell me what to believe."
- After months of talking with God, meeting with affirming pastors and faith deconstruction coaches, and reading books, blogs, and listening to podcasts, Sally began to understand that flawed theology and manipulated Bible translations underpinned anti-2SLGBTQIA+ doctrines. She acknowledged the harm her old beliefs did and is committed to her new role as a mama bear and advocate for 2SLGBTQIA+ people in her community.

Some of my clients choose to stay in church while they deconstruct, but the majority take a step back to relieve the pressure enough to feel like deconstruction is survivable. Trusting a new faith community is hard for most of us, but it can be excruciatingly hard and even traumatic for people who experienced abuse and rejection at the hands of their old church. For people in this situation, a period away helps them feel safe enough to begin lowering their walls and be honest with themselves about their doubts.

Physical distance from the church and the anonymity of online worship offers a layer of protection for those who are still tender from their #ChurchHurt. For this season of deconstruction, it may feel safe to attend services online and even send in prayer requests and support an online church financially. But few of my fellow deconstructors have found a spiritual home in a religious community that welcomes their questioning, doubting, and desire to dismantle oppressive systems within the church.

Many people who are deconstructing are not quite ready to give up on faith even after recognizing how toxic their religious community is. They still hold out hope that they won't always be spiritual orphans. Many of us don't know where we will land at the end of our deconstruction or even if deconstruction ever really ends. What we *do* know is that sometimes leaving the church is the best way to find healing, ourselves, and maybe even God. So, we keep the church at arm's length and engage on our terms. We worship from home, extract what meaning we can from online church, and long for the day we can once again be part of a community that nourishes us on every level. Until then, we will gather in the margins of faith communities, sit with the trusted few who honor this spiritual journey we call deconstruction, and do the deep healing work from toxic religion.

3

Pack for Your Deconstruction Journey

No matter how prepared you are for faith deconstruction, you will always feel unexpected experiences and emotions. By definition, true deconstruction should be unpredictable because you are exploring and questioning without trying to control the outcome.

Wherever you are in your deconstruction journey, now is the best time to gather resources that will support you when a high-and-inside curveball knocks you on your butt. I'll start you off with a handful of the most crucial resources you'll want access to during deconstruction, especially on the hard days. Think of these like tools in your toolbox that you can pull out when you need them. These resources are here to serve you, and you're under no obligation to use them in a certain way. Be careful not to fall back into legalism about how, when, and where you access each resource.

You Are Who You Need Most on This Journey

First (and perhaps most importantly), the most crucial relationship to cultivate during deconstruction is your relationship with yourself. This may run counter to what you learned from toxic religion. In this chapter I'm going to give you a packing list for your deconstruction journey; there will be some tools you'll need to acquire, some skills to learn, and some relationships to redefine.

But before we start talking about those external resources. I'm going to let you in on the scariest and perhaps the hardest part of deconstruction.

First and foremost, you'll need you.

All of you.

You'll need to connect with yourself in ways you never knew were possible, and that's going to require you to wade through some repressed shit you thought you'd hidden away forever.

I know, I know, I know—there's a really good chance you rolled your eyes and balked at the idea of a deconstruction book telling you to love yourself more. But my response is, *why*? Why the push-back? Where did you learn that caring for and listening to all your parts was a bad thing?

Chances are, you learned it from a toxic religious system that promotes compliance while exploiting marginalized groups. You learned to prioritize the voices of religious leaders and mentors over your own voice because they said if you were left to your own devices, everything you'd desire would be sinful and rebellious. Instead, to keep you and other community members safe, it was better for you to distance yourself from . . . well . . . the real you.

Here's the thing I want you to grab ahold of, even if you don't fully believe it yet: Locking away pieces of yourself never leads to healing. If you are fragmented, you cannot heal yourself or support others in their healing work.

So before you go any further on your deconstruction journey, you need to know that you deserve to find, reclaim, and trust yourself.

You need you. All of you.

Because there's a very real possibility that as you start to challenge and question, there will be days where you are the only thing you have to lean on. On those days, being connected to yourself might be the thing that gets you through, so commit to loving yourself no matter what.

1. Give Your Body Attention and Affection

Loving yourself starts with deprogramming what you've learned about your body. Your body isn't just a fancy zip-top baggie that carries your soul around. Your body is just as sacred as your soul and deserves to be treated with love, compassion, and reverence.

Instead of viewing your body as an object to be conquered, cultivated, and exploited, deconstruction invites you to reconnect with and cherish all the parts of your being.

Does that sentence feel a little too "out there" to you? If so, it's probably because modern western Christian leaders are really good at grooming followers to believe that anything taught outside the church walls is "weird and woo-woo."

Suppose you hit pause on that initial internal rejection of loving yourself by looking at yourself through a more holistic lens. I'm confident you'll discover that your body is loyal to you, and everything that he/she/they communicate is designed to keep you safe.

For example . . .

Instead of getting frustrated with your body for feeling tired all the time, sit and listen to what release or recovery is needed.

Instead of self-medicating to wake up, go to sleep, or numb out, ask your body what is keeping you on high alert and preventing healthy, natural rhythms.

Most of us carry around some heavy stuff we need to process. Unprocessed trauma, conflicting emotions, and deeply engrained limiting beliefs can be exhausting and overwhelming. Most of us don't realize we are capable of releasing them because very few of us were taught how to do this work. We learn to ignore our bodies when they ask for help and instead just disconnect. Deconstructing an old harmful belief system includes learning to love and appreciate every part of our bodies, especially the parts that are straining under the weight of unresolved trauma and screaming for our attention.

Commit to reclaiming and loving your body so that you can be your greatest ally. Start right now by shifting your language slightly. Stop calling your body an "it," and begin using the appropriate pronouns (he/she/xe/they/we, etc.). This serves as a reminder that your body is human and a living being that you cannot be separated from.

2. *Create a New Support System*

You'll need some personal support until you find the faith community that embraces your deconstructed belief system. You can totally deconstruct alone, but I wouldn't encourage that. As we discussed in chapter 1, faith deconstruction can be a really heavy journey. Having people, routines, and practices to support you will lighten your load significantly on the hard days.

When you start talking about your doubts and deconstruction publicly, some people will lash out and try to push you back into a tightly defined church-box. Others will pull back from you because they're afraid of what you're saying (or doing), and others will disappear altogether. If you've already experienced this, I am so sorry. I wish I could reach through these pages and give you a big, fat, mama bear hug because I know how deeply it hurts to lose close friends, family, and spiritual mentors.

Going through changes alone is brutal and not how humans were created to exist. If you haven't lost a relationship with anyone yet, now is a great time to develop a support system of people who are willing and able to hold space for you during your deconstruction.

When humans look for interpersonal connection, we often start with the question, "Who is available to connect with me?" I would encourage us to ask a better question, though: "Who has proven to be trustworthy and *deserves* to connect with me?" While this may seem like a risky strategy in the face of losing community, I promise it's a question designed to acknowledge that not everyone deserves to be in your inner circle. Seeing your deconstruction up close and bearing witness to your courage and vulnerability is a sacred gift, and not everyone is ready to tread respectfully on that sacred ground.

People in your support system should honor the work you're doing and be willing to hold a mirror up and reflect that sacredness back to you on the hard days.

I wish everyone we loved and wanted to be connected to could hold this space for us, but the reality is that most of the people around us are embedded in the same unhealthy belief systems we are trying to unlearn. There's a good chance that the people who raised you, those you go to church with, and perhaps even the person you're married to won't be very supportive of the work you're doing.

It's hard to feel like an outsider in these intimate spaces, and there will be grief as you create your new support system.

3. Expand Your Community

Forming new relationships with people is scary, but it may also be the most liberating part of your deconstruction. Just hearing other people say they feel the same way you do and have similar experiences to yours helps you feel less like this is a personal faith crisis and more like there's a broken system that is harming you.

There are two categories into which members of an expanded community typically fit. The first group is for professionals who are trained and paid to support you. This includes therapists, counselors, and faith deconstruction coaches (like me) who understand deconstruction and trauma recovery. The second group is for others who have deconstructed or are actively deconstructing. This part of your deconstruction community can form more organically or include joining more organized support groups and attending conferences.

4. Find the Right Kind of Professional Support

Let me offer a word of caution here about trying to recover from #ChurchHurt without a solid support team. Trauma is a brutal bitch who is going to kick and scream every time you take a step toward healing. There's a really good chance you're going to struggle with doubts and limiting beliefs that you didn't even know you had. Chances are also good that no one ever taught you how to change long-established behaviors and uproot those beliefs. Working with a deconstruction coach is a good option for most people, but combining that work with seeing a solid therapist will give you the best shot at finding lasting healing.

Scrutinize potential therapists and faith deconstruction coaches before reaching out to schedule an initial consultation. There are going to be lots of highly trained professionals who are also deeply embedded in toxic religion and unable to separate their personal bias from their professional relationships.

I would *highly* encourage you to find a good, licensed therapist who is trauma-informed and *not* connected to any church or ministry. I know there are good Christian therapists out there who can support your healing without allowing their beliefs to intrude, but I have heard story after story about those who could not. Those well-meaning Christian therapists did real harm to their patients who were trying to recover from religious trauma. So please, at least for this season of healing, find a non-faith-based therapist to help you without pressuring you to adopt a specific belief system.

Please note that training varies *wildly*, and there are a lot of Christian counselors, pastors, and lay leaders who offer counsel although they are not trained to do so beyond attending an occasional workshop or weekend retreat. There's an entire industry of pastors and laypeople calling themselves "Christian counselors" who are not licensed or vetted as mental health providers. Most are not trauma-informed and see no ethical violation in bringing their religious beliefs into your sessions. "Therapist" is a highly regulated term; each state, territory, or province has its own requirements for someone wanting to be categorized in that way. Check for a potential therapist's licenses and certifications to help determine the extent of a provider's training.

Many therapists may limit their practice to the state they live in (or neighboring states) because being licensed in multiple states can be expensive and time-consuming. As a result, finding a good trauma-informed therapist to hire can be challenging. On my website, I have a list of directories for therapists that is updated regularly. There are even a few fantastic links to lists of providers specializing in religious trauma recovery.[1]

Coaching is not therapy. Any coach you work with should know, and clearly be able to explain, the difference. The biggest difference is that therapy focuses on helping a person heal from events in the past and reducing the impact those events have on the present. Coaching, on the other hand, doesn't begin with any assumption that the client needs to heal. Instead, it focuses primarily on supporting clients to create the present and future they want. Coaches also do not diagnose mental illnesses or create treatment plans like therapists do. Instead, coaching relies on a co-creation model where both coach and client are experts with equally valued opinions.

Because of the complexities of deconstruction, I highly recommend working with a coach *and* a therapist, if you can make the cost fit into your budget.

Additionally, reconnecting with our bodies can be really challenging if, like me, you've spent years walling off the tender parts of you and fragmenting because of trauma. Working with someone trained in bodywork who also understands how emotional and spiritual trauma gets stuck in the body will be really helpful.

Remember, it's important to be selective about which professionals you hire to support you because you are inviting them into your inner circle. Make sure they have the skills you need and have done their own work so they can offer counsel without their own baggage getting in the way. Your time with a professional therapist, coach, or bodyworker should be one hundred percent about you because you've hired them to hold space for you.

5. Connect with the Deconstruction Community

In addition to working with professionals, it will feel helpful to connect with the deconstruction community. Hearing other people say "That makes sense" or "That also happened to me" helps lessen the feelings of isolation that deconstruction can create.

The tone and structure of deconstruction peer communities vary widely, but they're pretty accessible thanks to social media, blogs, and podcasts. Some communities are organized around a specific aspect of deconstruction, while others are simply people following the same hashtag on social media.

My best advice is to start with a few potential communities at a time. Follow, unfollow, join, or leave without shame. Remember to trust your gut, and listen when your body is telling you that people and communities aren't safe or aren't the right fit for you.

It's also wise to recognize that even healthy communities may come and go in your life. For instance, there were many social media profiles I followed and engaged with regularly because they were angry. In that season, I *needed* to be surrounded by people screaming about injustices because I needed to remember how to be angry after being trained for so long in "peaceful submission." I didn't even realize how much anger I was carrying within me until I saw strangers raging about the same trauma I had stuffed down and never processed. Their anger opened doors for me.

I followed the screamers for a while and worked with my therapist, intuitive bodyworker, and support system to unlock my valid rage and rescue the wounded inner child trapped in that walled-off part of me. After going through much of that hard work, I found that I was ready to move beyond feeling and expressing pure anger. *But* that only happened after I got really, really angry and grieved what had happened to me.

Sounds a bit dramatic, doesn't it? It might seem like I'm trying to be the Richard Simmons of deconstruction and cheer you into believing in yourself enough to keep going. I *do* believe in you, and you may get tired of me saying it, but I promise that liberating all of the "off-limits" parts of you is totally worth sweating out! So get mad and welcome the drama; just don't get stuck there. All of your emotions will deserve space in your story.

6. Choose Whether Christian Community Fits Right Now

Building a new community is essential to your deconstruction, and so is figuring out how (and whether) you want to engage with your current church community and spiritual practices. There's no correct answer to this question other than figuring out what works for you right now. I continued to attend church for a significant part of my deconstruction, and I maintained a good relationship with many of my spiritual mentors. But to tell you that my choice is the only way or even the best way would ignore the tremendous amount of privilege that white, educated, married, cis/het women like me have within evangelicalism.

My story is not everyone's story, and if it isn't your story, please give yourself permission to choose what feels safe and supportive and walk away from what isn't. Below are a few questions you can ask yourself to figure out where you want to set your boundaries and a little advice on how to answer them honestly within your boundaries.

How Connected Do I Want to Be?

Start this discussion with yourself by assuming a posture of deserving to feel supported without giving up your safety. If there are pockets of your Christian community that both support you and keep you feeling safe, you can continue to engage in those spaces. If things shift, you can always step back. Remember, not everyone you know and care about now gets to live in your inner circle. It's perfectly healthy to pull back from people with whom you used to be close but who are unable to support you in this season of questioning.

What Spiritual Practices, Gatherings, and Holidays Do I Want to Keep?

In addition to the expansiveness of God and your faith, deconstruction holds space for your spiritual practices to expand and take on new shapes.

Do you love worship but find that those worship songs you used to love now make you feel overwhelmed and anxious? Keep the worship practice and uphold your boundaries by picking new music that doesn't trigger your church memories.

Does taking communion still feel holy? Find a local church you've never attended, pop in just for that part of the service, and quietly slip out afterward. Or, you can take communion on your own. I know both of these options are considered heretical in many Christian spaces, but remember that the goal here is to stay connected to what's resonant without deepening your trauma by forcing yourself to return to harmful spaces.

What Will I Say When People Ask What's Going On?

This one can be super challenging if you regularly cross paths with people from church or if you're getting pressure from loved ones to return to your old ways. People who have shitty boundaries will not be great at honoring yours, so it's important to have figured out what you're going to say when people try to push right past them.

Setting your boundaries clearly is also important for the people in your life who are trustworthy but don't yet know where your new boundaries are. I recommend crafting two different sets of "canned statements" that you can pull out of your pocket when you need them: one to tell the trustworthy people what you need right now and a second to shift (or end) a conversation with someone who isn't able to support you while you deconstruct your faith.

For those who have consistently been trustworthy, you can respond with something as simple as "I'm going through a lot right now and questioning everything. Do you have the space to talk about that here and now?" Or you could say, "I'm asking a lot of questions about beliefs I thought were rock solid. Would you mind helping me talk through some of this?" or even "I'm deconstructing and it's really hard and heavy work. Can we do something fun that has nothing to do with faith, church, or heavy emotions?"

An example of the latter is: "I'm privately working some things out with God right now," or "I'm really digging into my faith to explore what's true and what isn't," or even "My faith just feels like a really private thing. I'm not comfortable sharing yet, but I will let you know if that changes."

The key to making these responses effective is to make sure they're honest and that you stick to them. If people continue to push, reiterate your boundary and restate that's all you have to say about faith at the moment. Keep in mind that setting and keeping boundaries are skills that are rarely taught in toxic religious environments; it will take time to learn how to do these things well. Be kind to yourself as you figure this out.

7. Create Time and Space for "All the Things"

Just like any journey, deconstruction will take time. Unfortunately, we can't add more time to each day, so that time to deconstruct has to come from somewhere! Because we are living in a capitalist society that promotes constantly trying to squeeze more productivity out of the day, your first instinct might be to keep doing that. Instead of assessing where deconstruction might fit into your schedule, you might just start deconstructing and plan to figure out where it will fit later.

As someone who tried to do that and has seen numerous others try to do so over the years, I can tell you it is an exhausting and brutal approach that stretches you too thin and leaves you feeling overwhelmed. Perhaps you're already there. If so, there's no better time than right now to be really honest with yourself about your very human limitations and make a different choice.

One of the biggest discoveries I made during my own deconstruction was that no matter how much I wanted the process to go quickly, I had to accept that *the magic is in the simmer.*

What do I mean by that?

Well, I always tell my clients on day one that unlearning harmful beliefs takes time. The older the belief, the more deeply it's rooted, and the more time the new ideas need to simmer before they become easy and familiar.

It's kind of like that old saying "Practice makes perfect," with the added caveat that in deconstruction, we can't cram all of the necessary practice into a tiny time frame—and we definitely aren't trying to be perfect.

It takes time to release the old hurts, to mother our wounds, and to invite the new beliefs to take hold. Our brains, bodies, and souls need time to sit with, wrestle with, and get used to new beliefs and behaviors. It takes time and energy to have vulnerable conversations about what you believe, question your relationships, and recover from religious trauma.

Not only do you need to put some time on your calendar for therapy, coaching, and any other of the professional support options we discussed earlier in this chapter, but you also need to put the time to simmer and recover into your weekly flow. If therapy or coaching is scheduled for forty-five minutes per week, for example, you'll need *at least* that long to recover and reset your nervous system after your appointment. Then you'll want to make sure you have time to think about and possibly talk about what you are learning with members of your new support system.

And don't forget your body! Your body is working hard during therapy and coaching, too, and your body will need some extra snacks, naps, and play to feel safe and well-rested.

Deconstruction can sometimes initiate a sense of brain fog, feeling slow, or not being able to do normal activities as quickly as you have been able to in the past. Give yourself grace. You're not broken, and it won't always be this exhausting to move through your day. You're dedicating a lot of resources to healing at present, and it takes a very real toll on your mind. Remember that you are human, and that's a good thing. There is no need to overcome the way you're feeling speedily or do that whole "fake it till you make it" thing. Both of those approaches would just reinforce old exploitative systems that you're working so hard to break free from.

Don't let old habits creep back in. You are calling the shots here, and you don't have to prove anything to anyone in a specific time frame.

8. Let God and Your Faith Be Expansive

Toxic religious leaders labeled parts of you off-limits. They said this was for your own protection because those parts were dangerous or inherently bad. In addition to harmful teachings about your self, it's important to recognize that they also pressured you to believe parts of God and your faith should be off-limits too. But it's worth asking: in what faith system have humans ever been in charge of telling the Divine who they can and can't be? Instead of focusing on all the things you "know" to be true about God, deconstruction invites you to ask, "What else might be true?" For example, patriarchal authoritarian religious systems promote a male authoritarian deity because that image of God aligns with their power structure and protects their hierarchy.

When we ask what else might be true instead, we find ourselves diving into the gray areas we were promised would destroy us. What if God is genderfluid and the spectrum of genders we see in humanity reflects that fluidity? Can you imagine what that line of questioning could strip away from your belief system and what goodness it could add?

It's time to lean into the uncertainty of what we really know about our Creator by looking around and noticing what is sacred and holy in ways we are not used to seeing. We are perfectly capable of expanding our view of God, the Bible, prayer, and church doctrines outside the walls of certainty that we were promised would keep us safe. (We will cover more on how to do this in part 2.)

One More Thing before You Head Out into the Wilderness

As you pack for this journey, you may feel a familiar stirring as your old trauma response gets activated. Whether you lean into this next phase of your journey with excitement, feel stuck in indecision and just stay where you are, or lean out with ambivalence all depends on how your trauma has shaped you. You are unique, and so is your trauma, but trauma responses usually fit into a handful of categories. It's also super normal not to fit neatly into one of the responses below, so hold them loosely as you read and don't pressure yourself to find the perfect fit.

Posture 1: Tightfisted Hypervigilance

You may be an over-planner who is ready to hit deconstruction head on. If you like to plan everything and clearly see the desired end result, it's time to do the healing work so you can loosen up that grip a little and stop trying so hard. In part 2, I hope to give you just enough information about deconstruction that you will permit yourself to stop trying to find the perfect trail through the spiritual wilderness in which you now find yourself. When you've got both fists tightly clenched around a perfectly planned itinerary, it's nearly impossible to open new doors, wrestle with messy ideas, or reach out and grab what you need.

Tightfisted hypervigilance is a trauma response I'm intimately familiar with, and I can tell you, it only *feels* like it's keeping you safe because you're convinced you can outsmart each threat that might come your way. In reality, you're distancing yourself from every relationship that feels vulnerable and walling yourself off a little more each day. Your healing work begins with learning to settle your nervous system a little bit each day so you can stop focusing on future things that might go wrong and start trusting yourself in the present moment.

Posture 2: Aggressive Resistance

You may not be thrilled about your doubts and you may be trying *really* hard to avoid deconstruction. Are you fighting tooth and nail not to deconstruct because it feels like your old belief system hurts less than deconstruction would?

Maybe in the near future that will be true, but deconstruction isn't just about *you* being harmed; it's also about ending the harm we do to others by reinforcing a structure that oppresses them. Tolerating an abusive situation because "it's not all bad" is a surefire way to ensure that system keeps hurting people.

Besides, even if you were the only person your current belief system harmed, you deserve to be safe and flourish! Don't force yourself to stay in an abusive system just to avoid fighting for yourself. You can do this, and you're worth fighting for. Your healing work begins with you learning that you're enough and trusting yourself to be able to navigate whatever your deconstruction brings, even if the cost seems too high right now.

Posture 3: Lingering Indecisiveness

You may be feeling unsure and struggling to decide whether to avoid or pursue deconstruction. If staying out of the fray has allowed you to survive as long as you can, it may be tempting to continue taking a back seat to everyone else's opinions and just wait to see how it all goes for others. Time is required to make big decisions about complex and deeply sacred topics (like faith), but there comes a point when not making a decision at all does more harm than good. Ongoing delay instead of making a decision is a trauma response.

Perhaps you find yourself here right now. Both pursuing deconstruction and maintaining your old belief system feel terrifying. You can see the cost of both, and it might seem easier just to stay in a state of indecision and see if this sorts itself out. You may even rebrand your indecision and instead call it a "neutral space" or a "balanced position" that values the diversity of people's opinions.

Avoiding conflict and never having an opinion may feel like tactics to keep you safe, but they're just reinforcing codependent relationships and self-doubt. Categorizing conversations, topics, and relationships as "off-limits" is not leaving you much room to live. Your healing work begins with settling your nervous system a little bit each day so that you can begin to find yourself again.

—

In part 2, I'll give you a loose framework you can use to start learning to trust your own opinions and ability to make decisions. This will likely challenge you deeply if you have been hurt deeply when you voiced your opinion or took a courageous stand about your deconstruction.

No matter what posture you're taking in the face of deconstruction, you now have a few more tools in your toolbox than when you started. It's time to talk about mapping out your deconstruction journey in a way that both honors your boundaries and your desire to break free from toxic religion.

—

PART TWO

Mapping the Wilderness

You may have noticed I use the phrase "your deconstruction journey" frequently. I have two reasons for making this intentional choice of words. First, because I hope the phrase serves as a constant reminder that this is *your* journey—no one else's—and it will be unique to you. Staying connected to that concept gives you permission to do it your way without having to justify what you're going through or trying to mimic someone else's deconstruction so that you know you're "doing it right." I've talked a lot about the individual nature of deconstruction, and now it's time to shift to explore the idea of deconstruction as a journey.

Second, I use this phrase because deconstruction is not a stagnant state where you sit still and all the "right answers find you. Deconstruction is a journey, not a destination. (Spoiler alert: There isn't one set of right answers. More on that later.) There's an ebb and flow to this journey that defies the rigid course you may be used to.

Deconstruction is a process that requires active movement of your entire self (mind, body, and spirit). Like every good road trip or epic odyssey, it's rare for that movement to be perfectly mapped out, follow a tight schedule, or go exactly as planned.

Welcome to the Wilderness

In a way, I hate to tell you this, because it may discourage you from going any further, but the fact is that there's no GPS map route through deconstruction. It's not a linear trip with a single starting point, carefully curated stops along the way, and a definitive end where that familiar automated voice says, "You have reached your destination." Deconstruction is more like a twisty pass through a thickly forested area where you very quickly realize you can't tell which direction you're going. That disorientation doesn't always mean you are lost, even if it feels like it in the moment.

Here is the liberating truth: you feel disoriented because you're challenging the old systems, routines, and beliefs that used to fence you in. Can you imagine how disorienting it would be for animals who were raised in a small enclosure to suddenly find themselves in their natural, unfenced habitat? Not in a little city park but an *actual wilderness* with millions of acres that haven't been cultivated and abused by humans? It would probably be frightening and overwhelming at first, but something deep inside them also instinctively knows they belong in the wilderness.

That's exactly what happens when we choose to step out of the "straight and narrow"—the tightly controlled enclosure cultivated by toxic religion—and ask what else is out there. Just like the animals who feel bewildered without fences, routines, and someone saying, "Here's what you will eat every day," you might find this level of freedom disorienting. For me, the wilderness was terrifying because I'd spent my entire life up to that point trying to figure out what the rules were so I could fit in, be loved, and be relatively safe. However, that wilderness was exactly where I needed to be, because in the wilderness there will always be enough room for *all of me*. The same is true for you.

Here in this wilderness, there is space for you to be you and to bring all of your baggage, your questions, and your wounds. The toxic religious community that raised you taught you that your emotions, desires, intuition, and sexuality were wild. They were right about the wildness of your soul, but they wrongly extrapolated that your wildness needed to be conquered and cultivated so that you could be "saved" from it. That's the part deconstruction helps you unlearn. The truth is you were created to connect deeply with wildness and be nourished by it . . . because *the wilderness was always meant to be your home.*

A Different Kind of Map

The deconstruction wilderness can certainly be put on a map, but it hasn't been and can't be completely planned out, and that's a good thing! Generally, people trying to get from point A to point B using maps are hyper-focused on reaching the destination by doing all the right things. There's an emphasis on *doing*, rather than being. You may have been taught to constantly evaluate whether or not your actions will move you closer to that desired destination or if they're a hindrance to your progress.

The wilderness map is completely different because it's focused on *being*, not doing. You get to put a pin on your map and say, "I am here"—and not stress over whether "here" is moving you closer to any specific destination. Tired of being *here*? Cool. Just start walking and see what's over *there*.

On your deconstruction journey map, there are *lots* of different paths you can follow, experiences you can have, and places you can visit. There are even a few options that haven't been created yet. The point is that *you* get to pick the path that starts where you are and leads in the direction where you want to go. You are a curious human exploring new territory, so your destination can change with you!

You can always hop off one trail and onto another. You can call a "do-over" and double back to a previous location. Or you can just set up camp and chill for a while. You can join communities, make new friends, and walk away from both whenever you need to without fearing for your soul. You can set up camp on a plateau, by a rushing river at the bottom of a lush valley, deep in a cave, or in a hammock in the highest tree.

You get to choose—perhaps for the first time ever in your faith journey—where you want to go.

The Vulnerable Exploration Flow

Deconstruction isn't a linear process where everyone follows the same ten steps and ends up in the same place. Even so, there are processes you can learn that will help you navigate this wilderness without losing yourself. Vulnerable exploration is one such process—a process of exploring what you believe with curiosity and openness, which is the very antithesis of toxic religion's pressure to live in certainty.

In the next several chapters, I will teach you a process that will help you ask hard questions about what you believe, explore why you believe it, and decide whether or not it's worth believing anymore. We will talk about why each step is crucial to deconstruction, and I'll share a few activities you can apply to what you're learning in the real world. There's also a note in each chapter pointing you to a resource page on my website where you can find additional articles, videos, and tools relating to that topic.

Remember, even though I'm teaching these steps in a linear fashion for the sake of making them easy to learn, this isn't a map you follow from point to point. Sometimes you'll do multiple steps at the same time, and other times you may choose not to do any of them. (Breaks are important!)

Last, before you take these steps, acknowledge the big, heavy undertakings ahead. Don't forget that you're learning to explore the wilderness that you were always taught was a threat, *and* you're working to get back in touch with who you were always created to be. Give yourself lots of time, take a breather when you need to, and pack some good snacks to stay nourished; this will likely take a while.

There's a whole lot of wilderness for your wild, sacred, holy soul to explore. Now is the perfect time to trust that the wilderness is calling you back to yourself.

—

4

Commit to Embodied Curiosity

For nearly all of my pre-deconstruction life, I walked around with clenched fists, trying to control myself, other people, and the outcomes of our relationships because I falsely believed this control would keep me safe. In some ways, it did help me to avoid certain bad experiences, outcomes, and situations, so I guess in that sense I fostered a little safety. But clinging tightly to the certainty I *thought* I had prevented me from having certain relationships because they required more vulnerability than I allowed myself access to.

In the early stages of my deconstruction, my fists remained so tightly clenched that though my beliefs shifted, I was still emotionally unavailable to those closest to me.

Fast forward several years to 2017. By this time I had remarried, started a successful online women's ministry, had five children of my own and fostered another child for fifteen months, all while suffering tremendous personal losses, stonewalling any vulnerability, and ignoring my own needs. My capacity to hold space for everyone else was full, and I was exhausted. My marriage was completely flat, full of codependency that was suffocating both of us, and on its last legs. Of course, most people had no clue about these struggles because letting my loved ones in enough to support me meant being honest with myself about how bad things really were.

So, I just clenched my fists and my jaw a little tighter and hoped that I could muscle through the challenges without being vulnerable or having to put in the work to build equitable relationships that supported me. But my doubts grew louder, my fear of abandonment and impending trauma exploded, and I walled off the tender parts of me a little more each day.

My closed-off posture was actually creating the emotional isolation, abandonment, and trauma I was trying so hard to avoid.

I got smaller and smaller while the load got bigger and bigger—until it crushed me, and I knew I couldn't keep doing life this way.

The Gift of Openhandedness

What I eventually learned was that I was holding too tightly to what I believed and even more tightly to the outcome I thought would be best for my family, coworkers, and me.

I wasn't fully present as a wife, mother, or boss. Instead, I was a fragile dictator with a walled-off heart, barking out orders. I was running from my wounded past and swearing I could make sure that I never felt hurt like that again. I was obsessed with trying to head off every possible mistake, attack, or failure. This kind of hypervigilance is a means of self-protection common for those who've experienced multiple traumatic events.

Dictators both rule, and are ruled by, fear and hatred. There's commonly a self-loathing or shameful core hidden behind the confident false front. I was no different. I held so much shame about my life choices and carried so many regrets about unhealed trauma that I mistakenly thought was my fault. As a result, I was still making daily decisions from a wounded, traumatized place.

Always trying to control the outcome is a common learned response to trauma. Perhaps you are also clinging to the outcomes you know you can "make happen" because that creates the illusion of safety in your life. Hypervigilance is about trying to keep from getting hurt, and it's a walled-off posture designed to protect your most tender parts. This means it won't allow you to be vulnerable, and, as a result, the heart cannot make deep connections with others. It's a fragile posture that requires more and more energy to maintain as you spiral deeper into self-imposed perfectionism and isolation.

Tightfisted hypervigilance is a learned behavior, which is good news, because *what is learned can be unlearned*. In this case, that desire to control everything can be unlearned by giving yourself permission to curiously explore other options.

You can't deconstruct from toxic religious beliefs if you're committed to clinging to and preserving what you already believe to be indisputable fact. Curiosity rarely leads to preserving the status quo, which is why remaining curious is essential to your deconstruction journey. If you are saying, "This is what I know and believe to be true, and nothing can challenge that," then you've already decided what outcome you want.

The pressure to always have the right answer and confidently control your surroundings is rooted in scarcity and fear, which are both prevalent in toxic religion. It can be hard to separate normal, healthy, and responsible choices from tightfisted fear because unhealthy church communities love the results hypervigilant people produce. When hypervigilant people are in charge of a project, the ball never drops, right? Think of all the little things that others would miss or maybe not do quite as fully as the hypervigilant person. The result is that person gives way, *way* more than receiving because that person rarely sets healthy boundaries or says no. Traumatized, hypervigilant people are so desperate for love, approval, and acceptance that they are easy to exploit.

That's why the deconstruction community is full of so many super volunteers and leaders who burned out, feel exploited by the church, and are on the verge of walking away from Christianity altogether. The deconstruction community is also full of people who have never labeled their experiences volunteering in church settings as traumatic but are simply wondering what they did to make those relationships go wrong as they feel them slipping away. Many people completely avoided dealing with their spiritual trauma and instead slowly disengaged from their church community.

If you're feeling really called out and thinking about throwing this book across the room right now, that's okay. Throw it if it helps. I won't be offended if you need to vent a little of that rage that boils up when you think about how much your past church experiences hurt. Just be sure to pick it back up so that we can get through this together. Whether you stormed out or faded away from your toxic religious setting, curiosity and vulnerability will help you find your spiritual center again. It is up to you whether that includes returning to your church or to a different faith community. The goal here is healing, not clinging to what you used to believe at all costs.

The Reason for Embodied Curiosity?

Curiosity is the gift that allows you to break out of the toxic religious box and move into a flourishing spiritual life. Embodied curiosity is the posture that will help you make it through deconstruction without collapsing into a pile on the floor in confusion.

The first step in mapping your deconstruction journey is to understand embodied curiosity and how it helps you break free from toxic religion. It may help you to take a little step back from your individual story to understand why toxic religious leaders get so freaked out by curiosity.

In this chapter, we are going to talk about why deconstruction relies heavily on our willingness to let go of the need to always have the "right" answers. Curiosity, rather than certainty, is the best posture for deconstruction.

Start by loosening your grip on certainty and giving yourself permission not to always have the right answers. There will be a lot of gray areas to explore, and many ideas in the wilderness will challenge what you've been told is unchallengeable. Be kind to yourself and remember that committing to embodied curiosity will take time and practice. You've spent a lot of your life being taught that pursuing certainty was pursuing holiness. It's going to take some time and a lot of practice to choose differently, but you can do this. If you are willing to pursue curiosity instead of certainty, then let's dive into a discussion about what you were taught and consider how clinging to it will keep you tied to toxic religion.

The Bog of Eternal Stench

That ironclad connection you feel between certainty and having a strong faith isn't something you made up. It's part of your indoctrination into toxic religion.

Christian culture highly values being certain, and it regularly equates certainty with righteousness—which, in turn, gives those who are invested in the Christian culture the motivation to "defend high ground from moral decline" when other ideas are presented. But just because something is taught in church and connected to Christianity doesn't mean it is automatically the moral high ground. In fact, Christianity and Christian religious organizations have a long history of perpetuating the opposite of morality. Christians have promoted some horrifically wrong beliefs and said those beliefs were based on the Bible. Many present-day Christians would now agree those beliefs were never, *ever* backed by God.

For context, here are just a few of the most harmful beliefs defended by Christians in the last few centuries:

Witch hunts. Christians were responsible for witch hunts, unfair trials of the accused witches, and the subsequent murder of over forty thousand people. Although Pope Alexander IV had banned persecuting people for witchcraft in 1234, accusing someone of being a witch was legalized in the 1500s.[1] Shortly after separating from the Catholic Church and placing himself at the head of the newly formed (Protestant) Church of England, King Henry VIII legalized witch trials in 1542 and kicked off a long season of brutal persecution.

In 1589 King James VI of Scotland believed that witches attempted to sink his ship.[2] Afterward, he aggressively persecuted witches. King James equated local healing traditions and folklore about magic with devil worship and allying oneself with Satan. In 1603, King James VI of Scotland ascended to England's throne, and thus became King James I and the head of the Church of England. With this expanded authority over both church and state, King James not only declared this pursuit to be a holy war against evil sanctioned by God, but he also positioned himself as the exemplary, pious protector of Christianity. (In case you are wondering, yes, this is the same King James who commissioned the problematic translation of the Bible that would be published in 1611.)

The resulting government and church-sanctioned murders of suspected witches leveraged torture, starvation, and nonsensical accusations against healers who were predominately poor women. Witch hunts grew in frequency and intensity across Europe from the mid-1400s to the mid-1700s. During that time, more than eighty thousand people were tried for suspected witchcraft, and at least half of those accused were brutally executed. Researchers have recently discovered that the number of accusations and trials "was highly uneven, temporally and geographically," which reflects the bias of local leadership and the way competition between Catholic and Protestant churches for people, resources, and political power fueled persecution of innocent people.[3]

Genocide and forced conversion. The Doctrine of Discovery promoted colonization as the best way to conquer and evangelize non-European peoples. This doctrine led to the genocide, forced conversion, and exploitation of the world's Indigenous people under the guise of mission work. Catholic and Protestant Christians alike have justified brutal treatment of people by calling it missions work (or spreading the gospel of Jesus Christ). In the United States, for example, centuries of the church and government-sanctioned initiatives destroyed culture and language, murdered and kidnapped adults and children, and devastated communities by stealing land and resources.[4]

In Africa[5] and Central and South America,[6] Europeans also deployed Christian missionaries to convert, exploit, and aggressively strip resources away from thriving Indigenous societies. More than twenty-five years after throwing his support behind the anti-slavery movement in England, evangelical hero William Wilberforce passionately lobbied the House of Lords to allow missionaries to "save" and "civilize" the "barbaric Hindus" in India.[7]

Today's toxic white saviorism is the direct result of the Christian colonialism that has successfully stripped power away from Indigenous people and consolidated it into white, European power structures.[8]

Transatlantic enslavement. Between 1525 and 1866, over 12.5 million people were kidnapped or bought, transported across the Atlantic Ocean, and enslaved in North and South America and the Caribbean.[9] While predominantly driven by the colonizers' hunger for free labor, enslavement was quickly linked to religion not only to justify its existence, but also promote it as a humane and compassionate practice that saved "heathen souls." Christians who benefited from chattel slavery touted the practice as benevolent and as rescuing ignorant people from eternal damnation by guiding them toward a more civilized existence, even if it was one without freedom and autonomy.[10]

Proslavery pamphlets relied on a threefold argument to promote the enslavement of people. First, the pamphlets stated that the Bible was God's inerrant word (that is, perfect and unquestionable). Second, they pointed to passages like the cursing of

Ham by Noah in Genesis 9:25–27, which the pamphlet authors believed showed slavery was created by God. Third, they stated that eliminating slavery would be heretical and immoral.[11]

Within the last few decades, the Catholic Church, the Jesuits, the Church of England, Southern Baptists, and several other American Protestant denominations apologized for participating in, promoting, and benefiting from the enslavement, abuse, and murder of millions of Africans.[12] While this acknowledgment is significant, many would argue it is long past due. And many, many other Christian institutions that promoted or benefited from the slave trade have not followed suit.

Segregation and Jim Crow laws. Even after chattel slavery itself was abolished formally in the United States, de facto slavery continued through laws and systems designed to keep Black people from accessing resources and opportunities or from accumulating generational wealth.[13] Thousands of acres of fertile land formerly were set aside as restitution for chattel slavery by President Lincoln. In 1865, his successor and southern sympathizer, Andrew Jackson, overturned the provision. His actions returned previously distributed land to pre-Civil War owners and stripped formerly enslaved people in the southern states of their ability to homestead and produce crops and livestock to sell. This essentially maintained the pre–Civil War power balance and kept the door open for other ways to legally enforce systemic racism.[14]

Jim Crow laws, a "codified system of racial apartheid," were enacted by Southern states and those bordering them to maintain white supremacy.[15] These laws segregated both public and private spaces like schools, stores, hospitals, trains, buses, and even cemeteries. Shortly after Black leaders like Senator Hiram Rhodes Revels and Representative Joseph H. Rainey were elected to powerful positions in 1870, there was a surge of new policies blocking Black male voters.[16] (All women were legally blocked from voting until 1920.) Paying poll taxes, passing a literacy test, and proving that a person's grandfather was eligible to vote prior to 1867 (which is where the phrase "being grandfathered in" comes from) were a few of the most devastating policies that sought to restore the pre-emancipation power (im)balance.[17]

In 1954, the South Carolina Methodist *Advocate* magazine warned churches to be cautious when considering desegregation because many white southern Christians used faulty biblical exegesis to pull scriptures out of context and support their racist beliefs that Black people, Indigenous people, and People of Color were inferior.[18]

The deeply rooted white supremacist beliefs, policies, and discrimination saturated every aspect of American life, including business, politics, education, law enforcement, and religious communities. This history is crucial to understanding that today's highly segregated faith communities are the continuing legacy of intentional segregation and discrimination.

Abuse and exploitation of "unwed mothers." The Catholic church created and ran eighteen government-funded "mother and baby" homes in Ireland from 1920–1998. Tragically, these homes were rife with abuse, neglect, medical experimentation without consent, and the trafficking of Irish infants and their mothers.[19] Fifty-six thousand girls and women from ages twelve to forty were brutally treated during their pregnancies, deliveries, and postpartum periods under the guise of providing care for the vulnerable.[20] This number includes those with intellectual and developmental disabilities and many who became pregnant while being victimized by clergy. Infant and child mortality rates in these homes was double the norm, leaving an estimated nine thousand children dead under these programs.[21] An official inquiry completed in January 2021 reported numerous ethical violations including unauthorized vaccine testing, placing children for adoption without birth-parent consent, physical abuse and neglect, lying to mothers who returned to reclaim their children, and burying children in unmarked mass graves.[22]

Support for the Nazi Party. In the early 1930s a movement developed in Germany to squash the influence of Judaism by partnering with political socialism and creating a "racially pure" Christian church.[23] Nazis presented the Third Reich as the heir apparent to the Holy Roman Empire (the First Reich), which fell in 1806, and the German Empire (the Second Reich), which held power from 1875–1918.[24] The Third Reich's ranks were filled with people professing deep Christian faith.[25] In short, German church members supported and advocated for the rise of the Nazi Party. The Nazi Party's anti-Semitism resonated with many German Christians, as did their rhetoric against 2SLGBTQIA+, foreigners, and disability rights. Even though Adolf Hitler privately despised Christianity, he proclaimed publicly that his party stood for "positive Christianity" and said that "by defending myself against the Jews, I am fighting the Lord's Work."[26]

Denial of the HIV/AIDS crisis. American Christians in the 1980s and 1990s joined in the mainstream condemnation of people diagnosed with HIV and AIDS and withheld compassionate action while the epidemic claimed lives. The Ronald Reagan administration, which promoted their deep roots in and loyalty to conservative Christianity, denied the existence of the epidemic until the spring of 1987; even then, the president made homophobic jokes during press conferences. In 1993, the Reverend Billy Graham publicly stated he believed God was punishing those with HIV and AIDS (predominantly gay men) for their sexuality—what was then widely believed to be a "moral failing."[27] His position wasn't new; it was the culmination of centuries of the cultural reshaping of biblical passages around sexuality to recategorize 2SLGBTQIA+ relationships as an "abomination" worthy of death.

Federal agencies like the FDA and NIH were slow to respond to the HIV/AIDS crisis, blocked access to experimental drugs,[28] and played down the threat of the syndrome with the full blessing of many high-profile conservative Christian leaders and organizations. It wasn't until the prevalence and visibility of HIV and AIDS cases in people outside of the gay community increased that the White House began to fund research and agree to call the disease a serious health threat. However, President Reagan and his conservative supporters never backed off of their position that HIV and AIDS were God's justified punishment of 2SLGBTQIA+ people.[29]

White Christian nationalism. The dramatic increase of high-profile politicians, pastors, and Christian influencers promoting white Christian nationalism also deserves a mention here, but I won't expand on it because we touched on it in the introduction.[30]

There are dozens of other examples I could cite here. By repeatedly intertwining politics and religion, many churches have embraced policies and stances that directly oppose the teachings and example of Christ. I'm sure you can think of some beliefs that are morally repugnant yet many churches still cling to them, such as the submission of women being a godly mandate, binary genders being the only "natural" options, consenting adult same-sex relationships being immoral, any type of contraception being murder, God mandating capital punishment . . .

I hope you're beginning to see the pattern. Each time that the majority Christian opinion was horribly wrong with regard to basic human rights and dignity, the church was (and in many cases still is) aligning itself with political powerholders rather than serving and protecting the marginalized. The church fiercely defends its correctness with Bible verses, sermons, and public support from influential parishioners.

Logically, we know it's impossible for the church to be right one hundred percent of the time. There might be hundreds of interpretations of the same Bible passage, yet each church would swear its interpretation is bulletproof. What I am suggesting is that embodied curiosity would be a much better response to some of the challenging situations described above. Instead of refusing to examine long-held beliefs, Christians have the opportunity to rethink their choices. But uncertainty can be scary, especially for those of us who have experienced church-related trauma.

If you were raised in or around the church, you were probably taught that certainty is close to godliness. Being certain, and sharing your ironclad beliefs with others, are considered the signs of a "healthy, confident Christian" who is perfectly positioned to live out the gospel. Churches that hyperfocus on evangelism, conversion, and increasing power by growing its numbers, push aside humanity's natural tendency to be curious because *curiosity unseats stolen power*.

When people face pressure to assimilate into Christian culture, questions like "Why?" "Who says so?" and "Are you sure?" become a lot harder to ask aloud. This is when hard lines are drawn. Insiders who operate within the system are categorized as "good," as long as they don't challenge the core beliefs. Those who operate outside the system who challenge its core beliefs are automatically wrong and seen as a threat to "religious freedom" by those holding the "moral high ground" in the system.

Getting curious about what you believe, why you believe it, and what else might be true is a huge threat to toxic religious organizations that thrive on assimilation. They are counting on you to want to stay on the so-called moral high ground, but their gatekeeping of what should be considered truth only creates a swamp of unhealthy relationships, harmful beliefs, and oppressive theology. Don't let them fool you with that myth.

The Holiness of Gray Spaces

Because you picked up a book about faith deconstruction, I'm going to assume that you've reached the point where you realize things are probably not as cut-and-dried as those in power would like you to believe. It's rare to have a clear right answer and irrefutable proof that it's the *only* right answer. People don't always choose correctly, and the sooner we acknowledge that, the easier it is to assume an openhanded posture and choose to hold loosely to what we know and become curious about what we don't know yet.

Adopting a posture of embodied curiosity builds upon the idea that there's usually more than one right answer to questions about life, and sometimes there's not even a *wrong* answer at all. Having a nuanced view of the world is the antithesis of and the antidote to toxic religion's insistence on absolute certainty and confidence. Embracing the existence of gray areas and no longer feeling the need to avoid them challenges the status quo.

Rigidity and rule-following tend to protect the powerful, exploit the marginalized, and allow abusive leaders to continue abusing—even when other leaders know it's happening. Curiosity is the gift that allows you to break out of the toxic religious box and move into a flourishing spiritual life. Being curious is the posture that will help you get through deconstruction without losing the best parts of yourself.

When we choose embodied curiosity, we have learned to trust ourselves more than we trust the people who are trying to control us. Our choice emboldens us to ignore toxic religion's threats of scarcity and accompanying fears.

Embodiment 101 for the Deconstructing Christian

Embodiment, in its simplest form, refers to *being in* your body—arguably a good thing, although toxic religion pressures us to disembody and trust the system more than we trust ourselves. Teachers of Indigenous wisdom have always acknowledged the deep connections between body, mind, and soul. The practice of embodiment is only an emerging blend of science and psychology in the modern medical realm—I learned almost nothing about embodiment during nursing school back in the early aughts. Fortunately, more and more scientific studies are proving the indisputable link between mind and body, and the importance of nurturing those connections through intentional practices.[31]

In the context of deconstructing from toxic religion, embodiment means disconnecting from the bad doctrines that say bodies (especially female bodies) are sinful and need to be conquered (an idea framed as being for our own good). Take a moment to think about how purity culture teaches that girls' and women's bodies need to be covered and hidden in order to prevent boys and men from sinning. Consider the value that's placed on a woman being "pure" at the time of marriage and embracing motherhood as a wife's highest priority—after meeting a husband's needs, of course. There's nothing wrong with choosing to be a wife or a mother, as long as individuals are choosing *for themselves* without being threatened by loss of community or facing public shaming or eternal punishment if they opt for something other than the expected norms.

These choices stop being healthy when other people (in this case, toxic religious leaders) apply pressure to convince us all to believe that those are the *only* healthy options and the *only* options that will please God. Throw in a heavy dose of if-you-don't-keep-your-body-pure-and-pleasing-to-God-you're-going-to-suffer-eternal-torment and there will be a perfect storm of self-loathing, disembodied people walking around distrusting their own bodies.

Embodiment invites us to acknowledge that our brain isn't the only part of our body that senses, knows, and communicates important things. Connecting with and listening to your entire body and self may be challenging at first, but it will get easier the more you practice. Embodiment means settling in and embracing the fullness of your mind, body, spirit, and the ways they interact that science doesn't fully understand yet.

Settling into your body can be as simple as taking a few slow deep breaths, stretching gently, meditating, or just noticing how your body feels in this moment, withholding judgment about how your emotions or needs may be hard to acknowledge at first. Remember, you've spent a large part of your life trying to measure up to patriarchal ideals.

Embodiment and curiosity are equally important because they are very natural parts of the faith exploration process. Without being fully connected to our bodies, sifting and sorting what we discover during our questioning of beliefs relies heavily on logic and conditioning and ignores a huge part of ourselves. By the same token, without curiosity, processing what we feel and sense within our bodies becomes more about finding new answers than continually exploring and wondering what else might be true.

The Synergy of Embodiment and Curiosity

Curiosity is an embodied posture, not a logic-only decision-making process. It requires being connected to our bodies, remaining open and vulnerable to our feelings, and asking messy questions that challenge what we believe in the current moment. Embodied curiosity poses a tremendous threat to the current power structure. Typically, individuals and organizations who wield power that doesn't belong to them aren't big fans of anything that doesn't uphold and defend the existing structure. Curiosity and questioning invite us to wonder whether what we believe is the only possibility. "Perhaps," Curiosity says, "there is more to this story than I have seen so far."

Curiosity allows us to hold space to unlearn the teaching that our bodies are "sinful," a teaching from the purity culture made popular in American churches in the 1990s and 2000s. Purity culture is a set of beliefs that insist sexual purity (as defined by patriarchal, often fundamentalist leaders) is God's highest calling. It is a confusing set of rules that elevates a female's responsibility to remain completely nonsexual until marriage, where she is then "assigned" with the responsibility of sexually satisfying her husband enough so that he won't experience any lust or be drawn to commit sexual sins (which are also defined by the same patriarchal fundamentalist leaders).[32]

On the flip side, males are taught that they're born with sexual urges and needs that women just don't have. In patriarchal purity culture relationships, men have the power and final say over everything, except for meeting their sexual needs and controlling their sexual urges. Managing those is the responsibility of the wife who, up to the point of being married, has been taught that everything sexual is shameful. In churches and Christian organizations where purity culture is taught, teens and tweens face a barrage of toxic, shame-based lessons about their bodies and strict warnings to avoid sex.[33]

It's important to note I am intentionally using gendered language here because 2SLGBTQIA+ people are not typically recognized in purity culture as healthy options. Instead, groups that promote purity culture prescribe praying harder, trying to do stereotypic male or female things, undergoing exorcisms, and attending conversion camps instead of allowing individuals to embrace a 2SLGBTQIA+ identity. 2SLGBTQIA+ people have been and continue to be deeply traumatized by purity culture's harmful teachings, but they aren't given status in these spaces.[34]

The shocking truth is that our bodies are good and were brilliantly designed to support and protect us. The harmful teachings of purity culture pertain to thinking about our bodies as bad in relationship to sexual behaviors. It is also important to mention here that ableism, or the belief that people who have nondisabled bodies and neurotypical brains are better than people who have disabilities, is a harmful, discriminatory practice that is also rampant in the church. Disabled bodies are often considered to be the result of sin, and prayer (or stronger faith) is pushed in an attempt to "fix" people who live with a disability.

When we are taught to disregard or even shut down internal conversations about our questions, we learn to prioritize what others are saying. It's easy to blow past our healthy boundaries and open ourselves up to exploitation that's framed as loyalty or love. We end up trusting outside voices (usually those of religious authorities) more than we trust our own voices, and we spend a tremendous amount of energy wrestling with and trying to reconcile what we feel inside with what we hear.

As we deconstruct, it's crucial to explore how our internalized ableism impacts the way we offer acceptance, belonging, and safety to ourselves and others. Deconstruction looks different for everyone, so it's also important to note that embodiment may be very different for people living within marginalized people groups. The way embodiment manifests for each person is just as varied as the wide range of human bodies, and that's a good thing.

The bottom line is that deeply connecting with your body is a basic human right. You deserve to love your body without trying to live up to someone else's ideal version of what that "should" look like. Embodiment makes it harder for people to undermine your autonomy and gives you a better chance of noticing when people try to transgress your boundaries.

The Unfamiliar Feeling of Embodied Curiosity

Perhaps you're already feeling a lump rise in your throat or a knot in your belly starting to tighten as I talk about gray areas and uncertainty. Why does embodied curiosity feel so wrong? If this describes you, it's normal for people who were raised in or around unhealthy churches to feel this way, especially if you were taught to fear anything that challenges the existing power structure. You may have even been punished or shamed for asking questions about doctrines that harm others. Instead of telling you to push past those uncomfortable feelings, I'm going to encourage you to stay connected with them. Embrace them, even, with curiosity, and let your entire body explore what's happening. In short, embodied curiosity may feel wrong because you were taught that your body is untrustworthy and that curiosity is offensive to God. It's totally normal that you feel conflicted because of your prior conditioning if that is the case. If you were taught to ignore what your body tries to communicate, welcome the unfamiliar feeling when you feel the tension set in. Don't override what you feel with a "logical explanation." Not this time.

Discounting our bodies is part of toxic religion's teachings that our bodies are bad and untrustworthy. To untangle from toxic religion, we must choose to engage fully with our bodies and learn, perhaps for the first time, what it feels like to trust the body we are in. Remember, the best part about conditioning is that, with time and practice, you can change your conditioning. No matter how old you are or how hard it feels right now, you can create a new habit of embodied curiosity.

Embodiment during Fear

If you're new to the concept of embodiment, your internal alarms might ring when you start listening to your body more. It's important to stay connected to yourself in the face of that discomfort.

Here are a few quick actions you can take to settle into your body when that old conditioning tries to take over:

Complete ten rounds of deep, slow breathing. Grab a comfy seat, close your eyes, and direct your full attention to taking in a deep breath that completely fills your lungs and expands your belly. Then exhale and try to release your breath slower than you inhaled. Repeat this nine times with the goal of slowing down a little more each time.

Change your scenery. If possible, get up and change your physical posture and environment. Walk to a different room, look out a window, or change your surroundings by moving to a new location. Don't grab your phone and start scrolling; physically moving to have a different perspective is key. Once you've changed your scenery, get curious about what you see in this new space by paying special attention to what brings you joy.

Move your body. Gentle stretching, walking, or tapping can help your body feel safer to be in when hard, painful stuff gets stirred up. Giving your body your full attention and moving what needs to be moved will help you reset physically when you feel antsy.

Cool off or heat up. Splashing cold water on your face, running it over your wrists, or putting a cool cloth on the back of your neck can help reduce those feelings of needing to detach from your body. Sitting with a heating pad, wrapping yourself in a warm blanket, or stepping out of the air conditioning and into the sun can also be helpful! Just experiment and see what works for you. Your body may not respond to cold or heat the same every time.

Trigger the good stuff. Fear can surface when you try to change your relationship to how you were conditioned, but those same mechanisms that trip old habits so easily can also be used to bring up new habits to help you de-escalate your fears. For example, is there an upbeat song that always makes you dance? A feisty meme that reminds you of your strengths? A dad joke that's not the slightest bit funny but somehow always makes you snort when you laugh? Keep those positive triggers handy for the moments when you feel off balance. (Please note: The goal is to reconnect your body with the joyful memories, not to lose hours mindlessly numbing out on your phone.)

The Benefit of Embodied Curiosity

Embodied curiosity paves the way for movement, and it's the antidote for the tightfisted, hypervigilant focus on fear and lack instead of on flourishing. Sometimes embodied curiosity allows you to move your boundaries to a healthier place or name your anger toward the people who deserve it instead of yourself. Maybe you're moving some kindness and compassion to yourself instead of reserving it for others only. These massive shifts cannot happen if your number one goal is to stay planted where you are and not be changed and shaped by this process.

Choosing embodied curiosity and loosening your grip on what you think you know will give you the flexibility to move through these really complex, messy topics without completely breaking down. Based on my experience and the experiences of my clients, I suspect the most challenging element is that this type of movement is about "being" rather than "doing." It focuses on moving your embodied, curious self through an experience. There are no tangible products created during this time—at least, not the kind of thing you're used to producing. This time is about movement and being fully present in the experience rather than generating something from which you can extract monetary value.

This type of movement is about finding your soul's rhythm and being fully present with all the parts of you. It can be playful and loud like a spontaneous dance party when no one is watching, or passionate and vulnerable like sex with a partner who knows you intimately.

Whatever image resonates with you, the key is that when you move curiously with your full self, there's nothing to prove to others and nothing to hide from yourself.

You can be yourself fully, with all of your gifts, talents, fears, and weaknesses.

Embodied curiosity unlocks a level of openness and vulnerability that many people have never experienced, which leads to the next question in the journey: "Why on earth would I *want* to be vulnerable?"

I'm glad you asked. Let's move on to that question.

5

Lower Your Defenses

Now that you're beginning to grasp the connection between deconstruction and embodied curiosity, it's time to have an honest conversation about vulnerability. If you've spent any time at all trying to fit into unhealthy religious communities, being fully connected to all the parts of you and giving yourself permission not to know all the answers will probably feel really scary.

In unhealthy systems like toxic religion, people are taught where to build their walls and who or what those defenses protect them from. People are also instructed not to lower them because disaster, evil, and darkness are on the other side. The constant barrage of warnings can make us feel really terrified of what's on the other side of the walls.

Before going any further, let me acknowledge that if those walls are built in an unhealthy system, then by design, what they're protecting is going to reflect the heart of that system. For example, if your beliefs about the presence and lasting impact of racism were created in a system that still benefits from white supremacy, the boundaries and defenses that feel most familiar to you will certainly reflect the privilege of that unhealthy system.

Unhealthy religion may have taught you that challenging, questioning, and doubting are signs that you're doing something wrong. They indicate weakness, selfishness, ignorance, or rebellion—attributes that you "should" work really hard to get rid of. Instead, you have to learn to lower your walls, de-escalate your defensiveness, and allow yourself to be vulnerable. Getting curious and lowering your defenses gradually will allow you to become more vulnerable. As you release your death grip on certainty, you can begin to release some of the things that are actually harming you as well. Holding curiosity in one hand and vulnerability in the other is what will allow you to move into deconstruction without feeling like you're constantly under attack.

It's counterintuitive to lower your defenses and loosen your grip in this season where everything feels like it's falling apart, but it's a foundational skill that will allow you to release so much of the pain you might feel right now.

Imagine if you put your hand on a hot stove because you thought it was cold, and as it's burning you, you keep saying, "It's cold. I can still keep my hand there. It's fine." No matter how much you try to cling to the old belief that the burner is cold and therefore not able to harm you, a hot stovetop will hurt you if you keep holding on to it. Trying to hold on to those beliefs actively harms you and potentially hurts others. You may have been taught to hold tighter to beliefs instead of questioning them; if so, you're wrestling with a learned response to different information.

You can't heal from toxic religion if you're trying to protect yourself the way you were taught to defend yourself by toxic religious leaders. Curiosity partnered with vulnerability will disarm your defensiveness.

Loosen your grip.

Trust yourself.

It's time to heal.

You can do this.

Unlearn the Old and Retrain Your Brain

Learning to be vulnerable and lower my own walls was the most challenging part of my healing during deconstruction. I had spent so much time trying to head off all the bad things that might pop up in the next moment. I had convinced myself that I was an expert in defensive anticipation and that it was a good thing for everyone around me. Here's the thing, though—those really effective defenses I'd built over the years were a mixed blessing. As I shared in the previous chapter, the defenses helped me avoid being hurt in the same ways I'd been traumatized in the past, but they also inflicted a new, different kind of pain.

Learning to lower your own defenses will require you to be fully honest about the nuances of what your life looks like with your walls up and your fists tightly clenched around your long-held beliefs. Allow yourself to move beyond the false dichotomy of things being *only* good or bad, and embrace the gray, messy middle. Your defenses have already done what they were designed to do.

Want to know how I know that?

Because you're still here.

You know the way you drop out of relationships when you feel unsafe or the way you use hypervigilance to mitigate perceived danger? The way you can't sit still because you're always striving to be better? The way you overextend yourself and keep showing up for your loved ones just so that they'll stick around and even to your own detriment?

Those are all very natural steps your brain and body are taking to help you stay as safe as possible. You know firsthand that bad things happen when there is little or no safety. On the most basic biological level, your defenses are meant to keep you alive no matter what happens to you—and they did that. *Good job, defenses!*

It's time to unlearn your old conditioning and retrain your brain so you can move toward healing and flourishing.

Recognize Bear Mode

Before moving on to specific steps to lower your defenses and lean into vulnerability, you need to have a basic understanding of what happens when we feel threatened. When you perceive a threat, your body's stress response is activated. Adrenaline and cortisol race through your body to speed up your breathing to increase the amount of oxygen reaching your cells, your pupils dilate to help you assess your surroundings better, and blood flow shifts to the essential parts of your brain and the big muscles to help you fight or run away from the threat. My family has affectionately nicknamed this stress response "bear mode."

The bodily functions that aren't essential to getting away from that metaphorical bear are diminished. Things like digestion, reproduction, and internal prompts to sleep are paused. While some areas of brain activity ramp up, higher-order brain functions (like emotion) are slowed or completely taken offline. Makes sense, right? None of those would increase your chances of surviving this threat, so these changes are a good thing. If there's really a bear present, you want every cell of your body focused on survival.

When you're threatened, most of these responses happen really quickly and without you consciously choosing them because a faster response time might save your life. You need this very natural and effective response to potential threats.

Bear mode becomes problematic when you slip into it even if the threat doesn't warrant such a strong response. Bear mode is not meant to be a long-term posture. It's a short-term response designed to increase your chance of surviving. This mode is so hard on your mind, body, and emotions that when you spend extended time in it, your body has limited capacity to receive, relax, and reset.

Toxic religious communities often rely on shame, manipulation, abuse, and the threat of rejection (in this life and the next) to keep followers in line. If that describes your experience, you have likely learned to move into bear mode faster because threats are always present. If you have learned to walk through life with your finger on the panic button, deconstruction is a good time to learn how to navigate bear mode in times of perceived and actual danger.

CHAPTER 5

Recalibrate Your Defenses

Keeping your defenses up, or allowing them to drop slightly and hovering in a half-defensive posture, is exhausting. You've probably already noticed that posture burns a *ton* of physical and emotional energy. It's time to rethink your defenses so that you aren't burning so much energy trying to head off threats that may not exist.

Defenses Distort Time, Shift Focus, and Reallocate Crucial Resources

Overly active defenses distort time and shift your focus to things that are not as threatening as they may seem. Past wounds may sit heavily on your shoulders although you haven't actually felt, processed, and released the pain. Instead, you vacillate between avoiding past wounds, minimizing how bad your experience really was, shaming yourself for "letting" it happen, building walls to keep you safe, and any number of other self-protection tactics. Unfortunately, these defenses prevent you from sitting with the terrifying root pain and you cannot move forward.

Your resolve not to get caught off guard again (which is usually tightly connected to the belief that you were at least partly to blame for your trauma) keeps you on high alert. Your emergency response system—bear mode—is always on standby, and it's hard to connect fully with your body or emotions.

When you're constantly on the lookout for signs of repeat religious trauma, your defenses remain in high gear. The majority of your mind and body are focused on what happened in the past and the present moment gets neglected. Your focus shifts further and further away from the moment you're living in until nearly all your resources are invested in avoiding future events and minimizing the pain of past trauma.

Toxic Religion Fixates on Fortification

You might be wondering why we are talking about lowering your defense system in a book about deconstructing from toxic religion. I'm glad you asked. Part of the reason toxic religion is so hard to break away from is because its leaders have gotten really good at using human defense systems to protect their position in the imbalanced power structure. Basically, if everyone is locked in and no one challenges the core beliefs of the system, it takes a lot less effort to maintain the current structure.

Just like embracing embodied curiosity, embracing vulnerability and lowering your defensive walls is *tremendously* threatening to the stability of the existing structure. When you stop focusing your energy on supporting, defending, and expanding the toxic religious empire, those within the system have to work harder to make up for the deficit you created. Alternately, the system may choose to let go of a little bit of power in response to your shift in energy, but I think we can agree that isn't the option they normally take.

It might seem hard to believe that a religious organization is threatened by one person's vulnerability. What I want you to remember is that nothing that's happening here is new. Centuries—even millennia—of conditioning drive leaders to protect their religious organizations. Squashing an individual's threat to the church is much more effective than trying to put the genie back in the bottle. Trust me, today's powerful religious figures are fully aware of how power shifted during the Reformation and Henry VIII's break from the Catholic Church. They're not looking for a repeat.

Attempts to protect the current power structure show up daily in the harmful doctrines, forceful evangelism, and weaponization of belonging. The way you protect core beliefs you grew up with is the direct result of the idea that "good" Christians—those to whom God is present and deeply connected—are solid in their faith. Having fortified faith (that is, having your defenses in place) means you are certain that you've got the core answers you need to receive God's covering in this life and an eternal reward in the next.

Not only are Christians trained to defend their own faith, but Christians are also conditioned to defend the church, church leaders, and evangelistic efforts as the best options to display that faith. Martyrdom and white saviorism are deeply revered in evangelical circles, so participants are exposed to these ideas from a young age. The more fortified a person's faith is, the more that person should vehemently defend the core beliefs in the public square. In turn, that person is celebrated all the more for "spiritual maturity" and deference to toxic religion's favorite causes.

Toxic religion's obsession with fortification forces layers and layers of rigid beliefs and legalistic practices to cover the curious, compassionate, and expansive spirituality that is more aligned with Jesus's teachings.

In the previous chapter, we briefly touched on a few of the times Christians and political powerholders combined and perpetrated great harm. In each instance, you can also find highly intelligent, well-read, charismatic, and devout Christians sounding the alarm against attempts to rein in the abuse of power. Why did they fight the critics if there was real harm being done? The simple answer is that toxic religion taught them to believe that their beliefs, and the religious system that greatly benefited from their compliance, should be defended at all costs.

It's the same reason powerful people at the top of the religious hierarchy claim to be persecuted when their abuses of power are challenged. American Christians have been told for decades that their ability to be Christians openly is under attack. Thus a leader can express concern about maintaining freedom of religion for Christians in the political sphere and in turn stir up the masses to stifle the practices of other religious groups.

Whoever toxic religious leaders consider to be the boogeyman in the closet may change, but the rhetoric of fortifying defenses is ever-present and undoubtedly serves those already in power.

Defenses Create Rigidity and Block Movement

The obvious problem with building up defensive layers is that fortified ideas, systems, and organizations are pretty rigid. Fortifications are designed to protect the most valuable people and resources, not to be flexible or evolve through time.

Imagine for a moment the biggest medieval castle you've ever seen. If none come to mind, do a quick image search online. The Mont-Saint-Michel Abbey in France, Alcázar de Segovia in Spain, Krak des Chevaliers in Syria, and Gyantse Dzong Castle in Tibet are a few impressive examples of fortresses. They're made of huge stone blocks and surrounded by one or more thick stone walls. Most were strategically built in conjunction with the geography and many tower above surrounding lands to provide the best view of any approaching threats.

Just like toxic religious organizations, these ancient castles have clearly defined layers with the innermost rooms being the most secure and the most exclusive. Outer layers received some protection but could be closed off from the inner sanctum if the cost of protecting them increased the risk for the elite inside.

Castles that are still standing have resisted attacks, erosion, and general wear and tear because that's exactly what they were designed to do. A fortress's strength comes from multiple rigid layers of damage-resistant materials surrounding the inner sanctum. The limited entry points, intentional pinch points, and closed-off sections of a fortress reduce the ability of an enemy to get inside those defenses and threaten the elite.

What fortresses *weren't* designed to do is move. You won't see expansive stone fortresses designed to be flexible and adapt to the changing environment around them. Once it's built, a fortress is not going anywhere, which is exactly what toxic religion aspires to as well. Immovability and self-preservation are the goals of fortified toxic religion, not the honest, curious, vulnerable exploration of faith.

But you, a living breathing human being, were not created to be an immovable fortress protecting the elite. You were born with a wild and curious soul that longs to explore. Deconstruction requires an exchange of ideas, truths, energy, and emotions. The deep, soul level of healing created by deconstruction requires movement, and it's really hard to move when your walls are up. That's why learning to lower your defenses is essential to healing in your deconstruction journey.

See, Honor, and Heal Your Tender Spaces

Healing in general and healing in deconstructing specifically invite you to let go of the hope that others will keep you safe and instead allow you to learn how to hold space for yourself. In this season, you shouldn't isolate yourself or stop trusting people. Instead, lowering your defenses is about learning to look inward for validation, hope, and healing instead of seeking it from others, especially those embedded in toxic religion.

I've spent a lot of time tending to my own wounds and mothering the empty spaces in my life, and I'm confident those actions were crucial to untangling from toxic religion. I have good, loving parents and extended family members who raised me with a lot of heart, courage, and desire to see people treated fairly. At the same time, there were also some things they couldn't give me because no one demonstrated those skills, permission, or gifts to them. There were conversations we never had because they didn't know I needed them, and I didn't know I could ask to have them.

Even if you can't quite put your finger on any actual trauma in your past, you still need to seek healing because toxic religion teaches you to feel deep shame about parts of you and to create division within your mind and body. You are taught to partition off the "good" parts from the "bad" parts and constantly try harder to "die to yourself" enough for those bad parts to just fade away.

But what if the "bad parts" you are trying to stamp out are just as sacred and holy as the parts of you that the toxic religion affirms? (Spoiler alert: They are.) These parts are just categorized as "bad" because they threaten those in power.

I rarely make absolute statements because I love the gray spaces and nuance in life. This is one idea I'm willing to share categorically. *Every single person* navigating faith deconstruction will have tender parts of themselves that need to heal—parts that long to be nourished and lavished with the attention they deserve.

Nourishing those tender spaces first requires you to lower the defenses that surround and protect them. There are a few key observations about lowering your defenses.

1. Your defenses kept you as safe as they could, and for that, they deserve gratitude. Are you proud of yourself for getting to this point in your faith deconstruction journey, or do you beat yourself up with negative language, negative thoughts, and self-harming behavior? Shaming yourself for doing what you could to get through the hardest stuff is a learned trait. This is good news: what is learned can be unlearned.
2. There's a cost for keeping your defenses up and that loss needs to be grieved. Being honest about the harm you have done is crucial to giving yourself permission to move into a more open posture. You can always share your regrets with others or make amends later. Right now, focus on sitting with yourself and getting curious about what your push for survival cost you.
3. Your defenses will always be there if you need them again. When those walls go down, you are still a human being who has been wired to survive at any cost. Faith deconstruction will not wipe your internal hard drive and start over; instead, you are choosing to lower your defenses to a level that's appropriate for this season. It's an adjustment, not an abandonment of what allowed you to survive during the hardest parts of your life.

CHAPTER 5

Introduce the Idea of Checking In

Before we saunter into the next chapter and learn how to gather new and different info, I want to introduce the idea of checking in regularly with yourself during your deconstruction.

It's probably safe to assume that checking in isn't a new concept. It's highly likely that you are used to checking in with others. If you are an employee, most of you check in with your bosses to see if they're happy with your performance.

What many of you may not do is check in with yourselves. There are countless reasons you might have learned to disconnect from your bodies and your own needs until they're screaming at you. In this book about deconstructing from toxic religion, the focus is on unlearning what that toxic system taught and replacing that conditioning with a healthier practice.

Now that you've committed to embodied curiosity and vulnerability, checking in with yourself can become a deeply spiritual practice to help you connect to your whole self. Looking inward and listening will increase your awareness of what your mind, body, soul, and spirit are trying to communicate to you.

Checking in is a sacred act of resistance to practice every single day. The steps of checking in are simple to understand, but be patient with yourself if they feel hard or awkward to implement. Remember, new muscles take time to develop so don't get caught up in judging or shaming yourself.

The first step of checking in is to shut off (or tune out) as many distractions as possible and find quiet. Tuning into yourself is the goal, so tuning everything else out is essential. Take a few deep breaths to slow your nervous system down and deepen your focus.

Next, imagine yourself folding into the center of your body so that you can move around to all the parts of you without being exposed to the outside world. Start by examining a part of your body that is calling for your attention. Perhaps your heart feels heavy or your jaw is tightly clenched. Imagine yourself moving from the core of your body to that area and asking, "What's here for me to notice?"

Don't rush. Pull up a chair and stay in that space until you feel heard. When it feels like there's nothing left to sense, acknowledge that part of you by saying, "I see and hear you. I value what you're carrying and am holding space for all of us here."

After acknowledging yourself, return to the center of your body and repeat the process with your entire body. It may help to follow a star-like pattern by moving from your core to the fingertips on your right hand, then back to your core, then on to the top of your head, then back to your core. Repeat this process with your left fingertips, left toes, and right toes until you've visited all five points of the star. Be sure to return to the core of your body each time, and pause to breathe deeply as needed.

Your goal is simply to notice and acknowledge what is going on, not to judge or change it. The posture for checking in is rooted in embodied curiosity, vulnerability, and self-compassion. Don't worry about interpreting, challenging, or learning more about what you feel or discover during this process; we will address those findings in the next few chapters.

This process of checking in will make it easier to hold space for all of you and acknowledge the realness of your feelings, even when they're hard, unfamiliar, or scary. Checking in paves the way for your next step in your faith deconstruction journey; you can gather new and different information without becoming overwhelmed or shutting down.

6

Gather New and Different Information

As I write this, I'm sitting in a small, gray jury room, enjoying a moment of alone time while my fellow jurors run out to grab some lunch. It's day one of the trial, and we just heard the opening arguments in a tragic murder case. With nine charges and multiple victims and witnesses, I already know it's going to be a lot of information to process. I stay behind at lunch because I know it will be hard to hear all the information, much less sift through it and decide whether the state has proved its case enough to convict the defendant.

I need to grab a snack, find a quiet corner, and check in with my body, which is already feeling a little overwhelm creeping in. After a day and a half of being in the courtroom, my body is already straining under the mounting pressure and escalating fatigue. Clearing my head and recentering is going to be essential to making it through multiple days of being surrounded by people who want me to believe radically different things.

The defense planted some seeds in their opening arguments to hint where they were going with their argument. During jury selection, the defense attorney asked a few prospective jurors if they thought "the truth ever changes" and (not so subtly) insinuated that if it was the truth, it would always be the same.

Not everyone received the same questions, and the defense attorney didn't ask my opinion on the never-changing nature of truth. If she had, there's a good chance I would have been eliminated from the jury because I know two things to be true about what we label truth.

First, I know trauma does weird things to our ability to remember things clearly. In previous chapters, I've talked about how nonessential brain and body functions slow down or even go completely offline when we are in bear mode. These shifts can deeply impact how we observe our present situation and how we store those observations away to recall later. Just because my brain believes something to be true doesn't make it true, especially in threatening situations where the brain's primary focus is on survival.

The second thing I've learned—the hard way—is that there are very few concrete, absolute truths. Most things we hold as truths are relative. Our bias, life experience, and intent strongly shape the ways we perceive and interpret the data in front of us.

Anyone who shares a living space with a partner or roommate who has a different perspective on where the thermostat should be set knows this to be true. Whether the temperature in a bedroom is hot, cold, or just right varies greatly based on what each person is used to and how their body responds to temperature shifts. If I say our room is cold and my husband says it's perfectly comfortable, who is right? Which answer is true?

Here is another example of the relativity of truth. Ask a child who is comfortable with clutter (or even total chaos) to straighten their room. Wait a few hours and ask if it's clean. You might get a yes response, but is it clean to your standards? Or is the room just cleaner than it was when the child started? Did the child lie by saying it was clean if the room didn't meet your expectations? Or are there two equally true versions of the events?

What we may consider to be rock-solid truth is often relative, nuanced, and can change over time.

CHAPTER 6

Your Definition of Truth Impacts Your Deconstruction

It is totally normal and healthy for our context to shape our understanding of truth. Examining our context is how we learn about and adapt to our environment.

Behavior is reinforced when we are surrounded by people with similar backgrounds, life experiences, and desires. We often choose, or are born into, communities of people who hold similar beliefs; the result is that we develop a limited view of the world. Our understanding of truth is restricted to what is called truth by the people around us. This is commonly called groupthink, and it's a dangerous but common phenomenon. The more time we spend with people who hold similar beliefs, the more we believe those shared beliefs are the best and most correct.

In fortified toxic religious communities, the pressure to conform and not rock the boat is exacerbated by the threat of public shaming, excommunication, and eternal punishment by God if you challenge an accepted truth. Our very human desire to belong to the community is weaponized to keep us from exploring gray areas and other experiences. Why? Because our community believes like we do and we want to fit in. Thinking outside the box is discouraged. Instead of allowing ourselves to explore and grow together, there's a deepening of commitment to conform with the shared beliefs held by the community, even when those beliefs are challenged with solid data.

As you've wandered into your deconstruction journey, you've probably come to the realization that *your truth isn't the only truth that exists*. Even though you may be confident in your own experience, it is a mistake to assume that others have had or should have had, the same experience. Often, this epiphany is the gateway realization that unravels other aspects of your faith.

Deconstruction challenges you to accept that what you know now is not all that there is. It invites you to look beyond the fortified walls of your current beliefs and ask, "What else is out there that might be true?" It's crucial to break out of the bubble of people who believe just the same as you do. This chapter explains the importance of reading and listening to people who see from perspectives you haven't yet (and might not ever) experienced.

There are so many confusing teachings in the church. You might have expected gathering new and different information to be the start of your deconstruction process. In fact, learning more about the conflicting beliefs within modern Christianity may have actually been the catalyst for your deconstruction. But if being exposed to new information was the *only* thing necessary to change people's minds, the majority of people would be deconstructing all the time, because information is everywhere.

Thanks to the internet, access to information is no longer restricted to the wealthiest individuals who are deeply connected to powerful organizations. While technology and the information it gives us access to isn't universally available, an overwhelming majority of people reading this book have regular and reliable access to the internet.

But instead of a widespread explosion of knowledge and learning, what seems to be happening in Christian circles is a doubling down on old beliefs when faced with new information that invalidates or challenges those beliefs. One of the harmful sides of the free flow of information is the proliferation of websites, blogs, and self-proclaimed "news" sites dedicated to upholding the current imbalanced power structure by producing exaggerated, inflammatory, and unsupported claims.

So here you are, mid-deconstruction, with instant access to seemingly infinite information, and you may already feel a sense of overwhelm and fatigue creep in, just like I felt in the jury room. Don't lose heart. In this chapter, I will explore how and where to gather new and different information. First, I'll talk a little about your responsibilities and posture as you move into this stage of vulnerable exploration.

Choices Do Not Equal Control

The most important thing to remember in this stage is that you are a seeker, not the author controlling the narrative. You will certainly encounter topics you didn't know about, disagree with, and just don't have the bandwidth to process right now. The resistance you feel does not mean those things aren't true; you just need a little more time to let the ideas simmer. That's okay.

As you explore, you're also bound to bump into some bias you didn't know was there. Pay close attention to what stirs up your defenses and how your body responds to people who are sharing their truths. Do you feel resentful? Try to center your own experience instead? Redirect to something less controversial? Or do you just shut down the conversation and walk away?

Getting up close and personal with your default defense mechanism is the key to disarming it before you get lost in it. Remind yourself as many times as you need to that you are committed to a posture of embodied curiosity and vulnerability. Bias toward your own story being the truth is the only lens you've had to view the world through. It's okay if you find it challenging to see things differently. You don't have to absorb all of the information you gather. Processing information is a future endeavor, but for now, stay here in the gathering stage.

The Pace You Choose Matters

For the purpose of learning this process, I strongly recommend that you pick one topic to focus on while you read the remaining chapters. It will make it easier for you to gain a deep understanding of this process and you'll be able to repeat steps with additional topics later.

Also, mind your pace. You didn't arrive here in one day, and you won't correct course in one day either. You need time to sit with these new ideas and really process them in your mind and in your body. Trying to do this work too fast will create chaos and pressure. Instead, trust that there is plenty of time to work through the unhealthy things you learned from toxic religion. Build in time to rest and play without forcing yourself to come up with all the answers in one sitting.

Pastors pack their sermons with hot takes on the tortoise and the hare, but the fact is that both roles are unhealthy for humans to play. The hare's style of sprinting and then napping, sprinting, then napping, and then freaking out at the end of the race when he realizes someone else is winning is solidly rooted in a scarcity mentality. Don't fall into that trap. It's going to foster chaos and competition and will build resentment in you toward those who are "ahead" of you in deconstruction.

But the slow-and-steady model of the tortoise isn't any better because it pressures you to *always* be doing something under the guise that it increases your chance of succeeding. Consistent pacing is great for a system that benefits from knowing exactly where you are at all times, but it's not so great for a human being who has varying needs and energy. You have natural rhythms that shift throughout life. The right pace for you this week might be exhausting next week. Learning how to listen to your body and trust yourself are crucial aspects of deconstruction because they allow you to set your own pace and adjust it as needed.

When you set your own pace, you shift your attention away from doing what it takes to cross some artificial finish line and instead focus on just being in the present moment. You're in charge of your deconstruction journey, and you're the only one who knows what pace is right for you in this leg of the journey.

Your Technology Use Needs an Audit

Technology is a double-edged sword when it comes to gathering new and different information. It puts millions of articles, people, books, and opinions at your fingertips, which can help you as you explore your spirituality. That same abundance of unvetted information can also be overwhelming and make it harder to discern which beliefs are worth keeping and which ones deserve to be forgotten.

When it comes to finding reliable information that is as unbiased as possible, you can't defer to technology to do the work for you. Typically, social media and search engines are designed to show you more of what you're seeing so that you'll stay engaged with that platform. The results you see are based on algorithms, which are very complex mathematical equations designed to predict what type of content you'll engage with in the present based on what you engaged with in the past. By design, social media reinforces your bias and connects you with like-minded people who share many of the same beliefs. Basically, social media is engineered to create more groupthink.

Don't worry. I'm not going to tell you to delete all of your profiles and go dark. For most people, it's good to connect with communities online. Instead, I'm going to suggest you leverage the power of the algorithms to make your deconstruction a little easier. You can't change the algorithms, but you can influence them to feature underrepresented voices on your device.

Start with a social media audit and shine a particular focus on who is showing up in your feeds. When you open a social media app, whose content do you see without having to go to their profile? Are they like you? Perhaps they are part of your faith community or deeply connected to your old belief system. Perhaps they are from a similar age, race, or economic demographic.

Examine your personal friends and the brands, non-profits, and public figures you follow. How many of these represent the voices of marginalized people? How many of these are actively trying to protect the existing toxic religious structure that you want to leave behind?

Keep in mind that pages and profiles you are connected to are included in the algorithmic equation even if they don't show up in your feed anymore. After scanning what content automatically populates your feed, go to the section of your social media account that shows who you follow. Unfollow all the pages that don't reflect where you're going so that they will stop shaping your feed in unhelpful ways. Go through the entire list of accounts you follow on all of your social media platforms.

Yes, it's tedious, but telling the platforms what kind of content you don't want is crucial groundwork to shift your newsfeed into one that is more supportive of your deconstruction journey. Listen to a playlist you love, pour a cup of your favorite beverage, and settle into a comfy chair so you can do this thoughtfully and thoroughly.

Your Feeds Need an Adjustment

Now that you've told the social platforms what you want to see less of, it's time to start communicating what you want to see more frequently. You can be nourished and encouraged by your feed instead of needing to constantly fight off harmful rhetoric that reinforces the old beliefs you're trying to untangle yourself from. You can use the power of the algorithms to your advantage by actively seeking out and engaging with content that expands your view of the world. Shifting your feeds to include underrepresented voices will support your deconstruction journey.

For the purpose of learning the vulnerable exploration process, pick one topic that you want to learn about. Keeping your focus as you work through the next few chapters will help you minimize feelings of being overwhelmed and allow you to build muscles that tend to be neglected and ignored inside the fortified walls of toxic religion.

Start by dropping a core question about your topic into a search engine. See what resources pop up. If your topic is understanding gender and sexuality, search for "Does the Bible support 2SLGBTQIA+ relationships?" There's a good chance you'll see lots of articles, blogs, and videos that connect to your topic from the old toxic religious perspective. If your topic has been leveraged for political power, the first few pages of search results will likely be from large conservative Christian media outlets, nonprofits, and thought leaders spewing more of the same message they have for years.

Wading through those results isn't the most effective use of your time. Instead, do another search, this time for the *answer* you're not sure of yet.

What do I mean by that? Well, if your topic is whether or not adult, consensual, same-sex relationships are prohibited by the Bible, then search for "the Bible supports 2SLGBTQIA+ relationships" and notice how the results shift to 2SLGBTQIA+-affirming sources. These new sources are the beginning of your updated newsfeed.

Pick a promising title from your search results and give it a quick read to verify that they're not an anti-2SLGBTQIA+ page hiding behind a clickbait headline. (Don't worry about how to process all the information. For now, focus on gathering your sources and exposing yourself to new voices.) Next, notice who published the article and who is mentioned in it. Are there books on this topic that are recommended? Are there any thought leaders or activists quoted in the article? Also, notice if there are movies or podcasts popping up in the results.

Goodreads, Amazon, and online booksellers can be great places to find authors to follow. You can use the same search process above with the added benefit of being able to read the book's reviews. Sometimes book reviews are more insightful than a book's description or marketing material. I tend to gravitate to reading the reviews with two to four stars because those typically have more detail than a simple " I loved it!" or "I hated it!" Skimming a few of the most detailed reviews will give you additional perspective about the author's position on your topic as well as other people's takeaways from the book.

Each author or organization mentioned is a possible addition to your newsfeed. Drop each name into your social media platforms' search engines to see if they are active on your favorite app.

Proximity to the Source Is Key

As you click through your search results, pay particular attention to whose voices are centered on the pages you're exploring. If you want to know more about how racism harms young Black men in America, reading articles written by a sixty-something, white, female professor will only tell you what can be seen from the outside. It doesn't mean that information is wrong; it's just shared from a perspective that is already centered in many spaces, and the purpose of this exercise is to find voices you haven't heard from before.

Instead, search for individuals and organizations who deal with racism firsthand. Get closer to the source and listen. People are actively telling their stories; it's your job to get out of your bubble and find them. Most social media platforms also have hashtags that can help you find people and organizations relating to your topic.

Don't wait for a white author in an ivory tower to regurgitate what people in marginalized communities have been saying for a long time. That only reinforces the existing systems. Look for people who talk about complex issues in nuanced ways, explore the intersections of multiple points of marginalization, and center voices of those who hold less powerful positions within our society. Pay attention to who is talking about your topic even when there's no big story or public controversy in the news.

As you explore, remember that the size of certain platforms can be misleading. Bigger pages may not be the best sources. In fact, in 2019, *MIT Technology Review* published a report that the twenty largest Christian Facebook pages were run by internet troll farms operating in Eastern European countries. (These troll farms also figured out how to leverage the algorithm for their own benefit by creating revenue, building target audiences for advertising, and spreading information to a specific group of people.)[1] Smaller, more intimate pages can be the best place to make real connections with the people who are deeply embedded in your topic.

As you follow new people, look for quality content from real individuals who embody perspectives you haven't heard.

Rage Requires Moderation

Let me start by saying that there's a time and place for surrounding yourself with people who are raising the alarm about impactful topics; sometimes, being around "screamers" can help you tap into the rage you were taught to push down deep. There was a time when I needed to be with people who were speaking out intensely against the same harm I faced, but that was a temporary season. It was not where I set up my permanent home.

Why? Because screamers activate our nervous systems in a way similar to bear mode, and a big part of your healing is learning to self-regulate in new ways. If your newsfeeds and inboxes are filled with people whose angry words can unexpectedly trigger you into bear mode at any moment, they're likely reinforcing the old habits you formed inside your unhealthy religious community.

Rage has a place in faith deconstruction, but it is not the only emotion that deserves space.

There's a balance to be struck here. We don't want to ignore everyone else's pain and lose touch with empathy, but we also don't want to pay attention to other people's pain at the expense of dealing with our own. Getting caught up in someone else's rage isn't the same as tapping into your own rage. The former can be super draining and will still leave you with your unexpressed emotions and unprocessed pain.

It is possible to passionately care about issues without allowing everyone else to dictate your emotions about those issues. Seek your own healing before you take on a heavy support role for others. Maintain your posture of embodied curiosity and vulnerability during this process; doing so can be key to navigating deconstruction without burning yourself out.

There's another type of screamer prevalent on social media whom we need to talk about. These screamers are powerful people who hold a significant amount of privilege in toxic religious circles, and they are afraid of losing their power and position. They're not outraged because they're marginalized and harmed by the current system. These screamers are outraged because an equitable society is a threat to the privilege they enjoy in the current toxic religious systems.

Even if you agree with some (or most) of their messaging, powerful screamers are not your people. They are leveraging their resources and position in society to pull attention away from the people who are harmed by the current system. How do you know if people fall into this category? Watch for people who fail to recognize their own privilege and position within the current hierarchy. People who cry out against their own perceived oppression, but simultaneously work hard to maintain oppressive disparities because they don't want to give up any of their own privileged ground. Their goal is to hold on to their own power, not to restore power to people marginalized by the current system. Having their voices in your head will *not* encourage you to stay open and value other people's experiences.

Get them out of your newsfeed and inbox right now. Don't give them any more of your energy. Remove them from your screens and set healthy boundaries with people who continue to share this type of content. You can always double back later if you miss a certain screamer's perspective, but I have a strong hunch you will feel better when they're no longer popping into your feed unexpectedly.

Remember, maintaining a curious posture is your number one goal in this season of vulnerable exploration. Staying open and connected to your body will help you as you move into the next stage of examining the information you're gathering and deciding what to do with it.

"In Light of New Information"

It seems fitting to share that my time on the jury didn't end with the discovery of truth. The jury didn't even fully hear the prosecution's version of the truth. During an early testimony from a deputy who investigated the case, new information about a possible witness came up that neither the defense nor the prosecution was aware of. The new information was a lead that never panned out—a witness who *might have* found a gun that *could have* been connected to the case, but the potential witness threw the gun in the river. The police interviewed the person and spent hours looking for the gun in the river and on the banks, but it was never found.

Both the defense and prosecution attorneys were visibly shaken by this new information. The defense asked to approach the bench to discuss with the judge and prosecutors, and the jury was sent back to the jury room while they debated how to proceed in a way that best honored the law.

As I sat with fellow jurors in the jury room and discussed what we had heard, I felt tremendous sadness welling up inside me. I knew there was no way the case could proceed. The defense team did not receive the information prior to the trial, and that was a clear violation of the defendant's right to access witnesses and evidence that would be presented during the trial. My heart ached for the families who would have to walk away without resolution for the time being, for the defendant who would have to return to jail, and for the staff who prepared so diligently for the case, only to have a single missed conversation create a huge roadblock.

After forty-five minutes of deliberation, the judge entered the jury room to let us know he was forced to declare a mistrial. He shared his disappointment that we were not able to continue. The judge let us know that there was nothing malicious or scandalous about the revelation, but the trial needed to stop immediately. To be fair to the defendant, all parties needed time to follow up on the new information.

Just like that, I was dismissed and my time on jury duty was over. I left with a head full of information, a heart full of mixed emotions, and no clear plan about what to do next. There would be no decision of the jury to render, no finish line for me to work toward anymore. Instead, I took a few days to be present with myself. I leaned on my personal support system while I felt my mixed-up feelings, recovered from the physical and emotional exhaustion, and explored how this experience changed me.

If that's not the perfect metaphor for faith deconstruction, I don't know what it is.

7

Examine and Sort

"I wish I just knew it was all going to be okay because on days like this it feels like I'm spinning completely out of control, and it's going to end *very badly* for me and everyone I love," Aj blurted out between sobs during a recent coaching session.[1] "I mean, I really love these new sacred practices I'm exploring that used to be off-limits. They feel so real and nourishing, but there's just this nagging fear that I might be wrong."

It was clear that the weight of that doubt was crushing one of the most sparkly, bubbly free spirits I've ever met. Aj grew up in the Bible Belt in a good Christian family. After years of limiting her beliefs and experiences to those her parents approved of, she realized she had been living an increasingly joyless life and disconnecting from her truest, most curious self. To get through it all, she had been unwittingly self-medicating with alcohol, busyness, and people-pleasing. These harmful habits helped distract her from the pain of trying to live up to the expectations of her parents in a belief system that now felt suffocating.

Aj moved across the country for work and then spent months working on her sobriety. She began exploring spiritual ideas, practices, and communities that she had been taught were taboo. I watched her reconnect with herself and begin to sparkle again by dancing in the forest under the moon, studying ancient feminine wisdom traditions, and spending hours discussing spirituality and religion with a local pagan group.

But even as she flourished in these new spaces, Aj felt a deep inner conflict over how so many of these experiences were considered evil and dark in the faith community of her childhood. When she shared little glimpses of her new experiences with her parents, they responded with fear and warned her that she was doing real harm to her soul. Even though she lived thousands of miles away from her parents, their words (and her conditioning from her strict religious upbringing) were always with her.

Just before one of our sessions, she sent her parents an article written by a theologian discussing the prevalence of witches and magic in the Old Testament. Her hope was that it would be a sort of neutral ground for them to talk about their different perspectives. Instead, a response arrived filled with multiple Bible verses and lengthy explanations about how Aj was headed down a dangerous road that would lead to eternal damnation if she didn't correct course. Her parents probably thought their communications were protecting her, yet they were creating torment and pain.

Her heart was shattered, and she was struggling to shake off their warnings. She was positive her parents loved her and was beginning to wonder if they were seeing things more clearly than she was.

"What if my parents are right?" she whispered between sobs. "What if I've got this all wrong, God hates who I am becoming, and I'm gonna end up suffering in hell forever? I just want to feel like they have my back while I figure out who I am."

—

Doubt is heavy. The fear of eternal punishment for getting things wrong exponentially increases the pressure we feel to be certain about our conclusions.

But like absolute truth, absolute certainty is rare. So what do we do with all the new information we gathered (as in the last chapter) if it's highly unlikely we can be certain we've found the truth?

The short answer? *Stop trying to find the right answer*. Faith deconstruction isn't a video game where performing the "right" steps will unlock big rewards and the next level. That's following the old system where things are always supposed to be linear, and we are supposed to use GPS maps to find our way to the finish line where God will tell us we lived a good enough life to rest in the next one. Perhaps it's simple advice to give and even to understand, but following it requires a longer discussion about what to do when we are confronted with information that challenges us on a soul level.

The examine and sort phase of vulnerable exploration is all about sitting with, and often wrestling with, the new information that you're gathering. It can be intimidating to have a variety of different information in front of you and not know where it fits, so in this chapter, I'm going to help you explore new ideas while maintaining your posture of embodied curiosity and vulnerability. This is a deliberately slow process; take plenty of time to sit and simmer as you make sense of the new information. I'll also show you how to carve out safe spaces to hold the information until you're ready to process it. (There will be more discussion about how to do that in the next chapter.)

Some of the new information is bound to conflict with your personal experiences and what you were taught was the absolute truth. The fortified faith structure we talked about in chapter 5 is rigid and immovable. Certainty is rewarded as holy and wise in many toxic religious environments, while challenging the cornerstone beliefs is labeled as foolish rebellion and sin.

You may have been taught to be wary of change and to resist anything that seems like it might encourage you to change in ways the system didn't approve of. Your old defenses may kick in as you ponder major spiritual questions. Emotional and intellectual resistance is to be expected (your own and others). It's scary to sit with information that was labeled forbidden or taboo when the stakes seem so high. But just because it's intimidating to challenge the norm doesn't mean that doing so is a bad idea.

If anything, that inner turmoil you're feeling as you tackle these complex topics is a sign that you are doing the deep work that can lead to massive spiritual growth. The new and different information you gathered in the last chapter may change you if you continue to sit with it in a posture of embodied curiosity and vulnerability.

Remember to unclench your fists a little and hold things loosely while you explore. Clinging tightly to what you thought was truth is a posture rooted in scarcity and fear. You don't have to do that anymore because *you're* calling the shots here. Open your hands so you can stay anchored in yourself and not feel pulled in every direction each time you discover a new perspective.

Keep leaning into those gray areas. Trust that you have everything you need to keep yourself safe in this season. You can do this, even if no one else thinks you're on the right track.

"Holy Buckets, Batman!"

Before I dive into how to examine the information you've gathered, take a few minutes to set up the "buckets" you'll sort ideas and beliefs into after examining them.

You may recognize this system of sorting if you've ever watched an episode of *Hoarders*, *The Life-Changing Magic of Tidying Up* with Marie Kondo, or pretty much any other show where the home organization experts help people sort through their clutter. Designating a few distinct buckets that you can use to put things into reduces the overwhelm and helps you to stay focused.

In faith deconstruction and unlike those shows, however, there's no pressure to sort every belief out right now or to get rid of all the things that don't fit. The buckets aren't as rigid or tightly controlled by others as they are on TV, and there are more options than the traditional "keep," "trash," and "donate" labels. There's also a lot more nuance in your sorting. It's normal and healthy for some things to fit in more than one bucket at a time. In fact, if you could stand over your buckets and see them from above, they would probably look like an asymmetrical version of the Olympic Rings with circles that bump into each other and overlap in some places.

You get to create a bucket of ideas to keep. This is for ideas that you are curious about and want to explore more, ideas that you simply want more information on, and ideas that don't line up with what you were taught.

Remember, the goal of the buckets is to designate flexible space to put these ideas you're wrestling with so that you don't have to carry them around in the front of your brain all the time. Constantly thinking about these challenging topics is exhausting, and I don't want that for you. Rather, these buckets are for your benefit. They are flexible buckets, not hard rules that you have to stick to or else face eternal punishment. Establish them in a way that feels nurturing, supportive, and empowering, not legalistic or restrictive.

Use pages in a journal or stick giant sticky notes on your wall to lay out your buckets. Drawing them is important because it stimulates your brain in multiple ways to grab hold of the idea that these buckets are here for you when you need them. You may want to borrow Aj's response to this process: "Holy buckets, Batman!"

As I mentioned above, there are a few must-have buckets:

Revisit: This bucket is for information that you are curious about and want to explore more.

Keep: This bucket is for information that feels resonant and you want to lean into.

I Don't Know (IDK): This bucket is for information that you have no idea what to do with right now.

Release: This bucket is for information that no longer fits and you need to let go of.

This is *your* system, so you can change the names and add or remove buckets as you see fit, but here's a word of caution: There's a reason that TV shows about decluttering only offer people a few choices for their sorting categories. Keeping it simple is essential to actually getting through the process of storing. A simple system requires less focus and energy from you so that you can stay concentrated on the new information and what's happening in your body in response to it.

You could create a massive bucket system of twenty buckets with a more nuanced labeling system, but that means that every time you examine new and different information, you have twenty possible buckets to plunk that info into instead of four. At a minimum, you'll probably examine a handful of articles, podcasts, or books about each topic. Multiply that by dozens of complex topics, and suddenly you're making hundreds, if not thousands, of decisions about where the ideas belong.

This sorting process can become really overwhelming really quickly, so my suggestion (drawn from my personal experience) is to start with no more than five buckets and get comfortable using them. Once those sorting muscles are built, if you keep encountering ideas that seem like they belong in a bucket you haven't created yet, add a new bucket. Just be slow to add and keep your system as simple as possible.

Once you've created your first buckets, it's time to dive into examining the information you gathered on your topic.

Notice How It Lands

Check in with yourself before diving into your topic. I want you to be both fully present and fully connected to your body. This is a great time to remind yourself that you're committed to embodied curiosity and vulnerability while you examine the new resources you've found. Remind yourself that though this new information may challenge you and make you feel threatened, you are physically safe in your current environment. The person sharing new information isn't in your space; your response is private at this stage.

After you've taken as much time as needed to settle in, you can take your first pass over the material by examining it with curiosity and your walls down. To begin, pick a smaller piece of content like an article, short podcast, or video. A single chapter of a book or scene from a movie would be okay. Just keep it short so you don't get overwhelmed and give up.

Read, watch, or listen to the new information with the primary goal of absorbing it. You aren't under any pressure to make decisions right now; this is a judgment-free zone.

What's happening in your body as you take this first pass? Notice where you feel threatened, bored, excited, or anxious. What thoughts and feelings are coming to mind? Is this new information stirring up any memories of past conversations on this topic?

Remember, you're in charge of your pace during this first pass. You can hit pause, get up and move, grab a snack, cry, laugh, or do whatever feels resonant (even if it doesn't really make sense to you at the time).

Before taking a second pass over the material, grab your journal and jot down your observations about how it felt to explore this topic. Don't worry about sorting right now; that step will happen in a minute. Trust yourself to know what to do when it's time.

Become Curiouser and Curiouser

Multiple passes over new information are essential—especially early on when you're learning the process and when you tackle topics that feel hardest or most controversial. Those are typically the topics the church has used to exclude people or to gain political, financial, or cultural power.

The first pass is less about understanding the material you're consuming than it is about noticing what's happening in your body when confronted with new ideas. You're learning about *being* with new information and noticing how it impacts you when you don't immediately jump into *doing* something with or about it. Subsequent passes are for deepening your understanding of the content with embodied curiosity. Reading, listening to, or watching material more than once allows you to notice what's happening inside you and then process it. After the first pass, you can engage more deeply with the actual content without your defenses (which might have been triggered by any unprocessed stuff that came up during the first pass) getting in your way.

During the second pass, you've managed your initial response and now you can get really curious about what you're exploring. Continue to notice what's happening in your body, but devote the majority of your energy toward engaging with the new information.

The best tool I've ever used during vulnerable exploration is asking curious questions that are open-ended, short, and disarm the quippy, well-practiced responses fortified faith leaders adore. That's a mouthful, and it may seem complicated, but coming up with these types of curious questions is much easier than you think. Start with a question that's open-ended (can't be answered with a yes or no), doesn't push you toward a predetermined opinion, and doesn't avoid challenging your old or current beliefs.

Here are a few questions to get you started and an example of when you might find each question useful.

- What's that about? (When you feel something stirring inside you.)
- How is that landing with me? (When you aren't sure what to do with something.)
- What am I not seeing here? (When something doesn't make sense or feel real.)
- How is that different from what I thought? (When confronted with something you've never experienced.)
- What am I holding tightly to? (When you feel conflict or resistance to new info.)
- What might that feel like? (When trying to understand someone else's story.)

As with everything in this faith deconstruction process, don't let this become legalistic or forced. These questions and situations are examples to help you get started. Don't force yourself to use them all every time you examine new information.

I'm confident you'll create your own questions soon, and they'll be exactly what you need at that moment. Trust those questions. Trust yourself. Lean into your intuition. Anchor yourself in what your gut knows to be true, even if you're not sure how it fits right now.

You have everything you need to explore these topics in new ways.

Embrace the Conflict

You may be cringing at the idea of embracing conflict, especially in this tender season of deconstruction, but please hear me out. Conflict is inevitable in deconstruction.

Vulnerable exploration will create conflict between what you used to believe and the new and different information that's right in front of you. There will be some inner turmoil as you wrestle with your old story and the possibilities that are unfolding in the present moment. The thing you may not realize yet is that conflict is one of the greatest gifts of deconstruction. I don't say this because I love fighting; I don't. Sometimes conflict terrifies me, but what I've learned over the years is that conflict is an opportunity to examine myself under pressure. It regularly reveals tender spaces that need mothering, old habits that no longer serve me, and heavy things that are smothering my soul.

You don't have to love conflict to understand it's a powerful ally that you can leverage to untangle yourself from the trauma, limiting beliefs, and past experiences that may have (at one time) convinced you to take up as little space as possible. Pressure makes people uncomfortable enough to change long-standing beliefs and habits, and that pressure often comes from conflict.

As you sort new ideas and information, don't shy away from conflict or assume that it's a sign that you're messing up this process. *This process is designed to create conflict because it's good, healthy, and necessary if you're going to untangle from toxic religion.* It's way better to do this in the safety of your own home than it is to avoid the conflict until you reach a point of boiling-over and the repressed conflict blows up.

Get Your Shit Sorted

After reading, listening to, or watching your new information at least twice, the next step is to sort this new information.

Pull out your journal or sticky note buckets and jot down some of the ideas that came up while examining your new info. Stay connected to your body and stay as far away from self-criticism as possible. You can write as little or as much as you like about the new information in your buckets. Some people find it helpful to write long paragraphs; others, like me, find bullet points and shorthand more resonant.

If you're not sure where something belongs, include it in the IDK bucket and come back to it later. Release yourself from the pressure to find the "right" or "perfect" answer. Nothing about this sorting activity is permanent. You can always change your mind later if your feelings change or you learn additional information that completely shifts your opinion. In fact, you might want to plan on that happening, because it most certainly will, based on my experience!

As you sort, keep the reminder about setting your own pace in mind. There's no finish line here. This is just a process that holds as much space as you need to explore this topic. Be intentional about finding the rhythm you need right now in this season of examining and sorting. There's value in jotting things down quickly when they come up and sitting extensively with your thoughts so they can develop. This is a both/and process where there is flexibility to move in a way that's nurturing and supportive instead of trying to match someone else's pace.

Learn to Take the Win

If you're a recovering overachiever and people pleaser like me, I need to tell you to stop and take a break. Bask in the glow of the new information you sorted and celebrate the work you've done up to this point. Resist the urge to rush to the next phase. You are creating new habits, which require new neural pathways to develop, which takes time and practice.

Like Aj discovered, deconstruction can be brutally lonely, especially in moments when supportive words from the people we love can be hard to come by. These are the moments you need to support yourself and celebrate every single victory. Especially celebrate the wins that happen in private, where no one knows how hard you're working and how much progress you're making.

Give these buckets of new info time to rest before hopping into the next chapter, where I will share what to do with your buckets. You've done what needs to be done for now, and rushing into the next step without taking a beat is likely rooted in the fear of not having certainty. It's time to get comfortable with *not* having all the answers and *not* knowing where all the pieces fit right now. It's time to step away, take a break, and celebrate how courageous you are before launching into the next stage. Nourish yourself, have a snack, try some gentle movement, curl up with a favorite movie, and fill up your own cup so you can keep going.

8

Reconcile and Release

In the late spring of 2019, a dear friend (who is also the first life coach I ever worked with) hosted a small women's retreat near Lake Michigan, near a stretch of the shore I grew up visiting. Honestly, I didn't know much about what we would be doing when I signed up at the last minute, but there was a scholarship to fund my attendance, and I trusted my friend to create a safe and nurturing space. I also knew that space would calm my nervous system a bit and invite me to lower my walls. *This will be a good way to recharge*, I thought to myself as I registered.

I really needed someone to hold space for me at that time, because life at home was exhausting. The courts had begun the process of reunifying our foster child, whom I'll call Fia with her parents. Fia's visits with her parents grew longer, more frequent, less supervised, and closer to the parents' home—which also meant that the time leading up to the visits and immediately following them became more complex. My family was living in the strange limbo of trying to support Fia while she pulled away from us to make more emotional room to rebuild the relationship with her parents. Reunification had always been the goal of Child Protective Services. Although our caseworker had told us for months that it was unlikely, reunification suddenly became imminent.

The next weekend I packed a bag and headed to the big lake for three much-needed days of someone else being in charge. At home and at work, I was always calling the shots; I needed someone else behind the wheel at the moment, and a long weekend of not being the primary adult in charge of anything sounded like a relief.

As I expected, it turned out to be a weekend packed with opportunities to be vulnerable and activities designed to draw me closer to my very wounded and tender body. As we neared the end of our time together, the other attendees and I gathered in the living room of our vacation rental and shared our thoughts about our most vulnerable spaces. When it was my turn to talk, a lump rose in my throat and nearly choked me.

"It seems like 'fierce' has been my word for the last fifteen years," I sputtered with a tense, tightly controlled voice. "I am really good at fiercely fighting for people, but I don't know how to do this. I don't know how to let Fia go back when I know she'd have more support, stability, and opportunities with us. But I also know she might never heal from this whole thing if she doesn't get to go home. I want to support her and send her home without adding more trauma by pulling away before she goes."

By this point, my words were practically whispers, and it physically hurt me to be this open with people I did not know well. I was terrified to be this honest with them and with myself.

"It's breaking my heart in so many different ways, and my husband and kiddos are grieving too," I stammered. "No one prepared me for this, and I just don't know how to fiercely release."

The women sitting in the circle quietly nodded, and tears formed in a few eyes. My pain made sense to them because they were healers, leaders, moms, and strong women too. They understood the complexity of loving someone this much, and the pain of knowing that letting that person go was the other person's best chance of finding happiness.

I was struggling to release the belief that Fia staying with us would be the best thing for her. My heart wanted to keep fighting, to say that she deserves better, and to protect my family from the grief of the impending loss. This situation was also activating my deepest fears of abandonment, not being good enough, and being rejected by those closest to me. I felt like there was no good answer: She was going to lose some people no matter what, and it seemed like the best option for her was to go home to her biological parents.

I was at a point where reconciliation and release were desperately needed, but it felt like they were going to break me in ways I would never be able to heal.

Analyzing Beliefs and Belief Systems

In this phase—where you are right now on your deconstruction journey—your goal is to find alignment, not to avoid conflict or create ease in your life. There will be peace and ease later, but right now, you're in the midst of wrestling and emotional heavy lifting.

As you seek to reconcile the old and the new, it's important to stay clear of the false dichotomy of absolutes. This is the perfect season to embrace the gray areas and expand the nuance of your beliefs. Give in to the inevitability of your I Don't Know bucket never emptying all the way because there will always be more out there to explore.

Having head knowledge is only one aspect of deconstruction. This process also transforms our deepest beliefs and our daily actions. It's a season of rooting out the beliefs that are out of alignment so that your behaviors will reflect your deconstructed belief system. While it sounds simple, this may be one of the most grueling seasons of your deconstruction journey because it's time to make some decisions about what you want to hold on to and how that will play out in your daily life.

Your belief system is made up of all the things you know, value, and want to honor and connect to during the day-to-day. The individual beliefs within this system are built around ideas you believe to be true. Some are deeply connected to core truths you hold as unchallengeable. These beliefs are the ones at the center of your daily actions. When you feel your defenses rise, there's a good chance one of these core beliefs has been stepped on. It's likely that much of what you have been taught about Christianity is categorized as a core belief, which is why deconstructing your faith completely rocks your sense of who you are.

Spiritual beliefs in particular are deeply personal and intimate. They're tightly connected to your hopes and dreams for your life, and that's why you cling to them so tightly. Beliefs are typically cultivated over a lifetime, and shifting them can stir up significant feelings of insecurity and fears of making wrong decisions.

There's a good chance that the people around you have similar core beliefs, because shared core beliefs give us a strong foundation to create relationships that feel safe and in alignment with what matters most to us. Other beliefs are peripheral and less central to your core identity. Peripheral beliefs still matter to you, and you may defend them at times, but because they're not as essential to your well-being, you probably hold them a little more loosely and aren't nearly as agitated when they are challenged. Peripheral beliefs also shift more easily when you encounter new ideas.

Responding When Beliefs Are Challenged

How we respond when our values or beliefs are being challenged varies widely based on how important that value is, how much we trust the person issuing the challenge, and how vulnerable we feel in the relationship. Sometimes being challenged is not a big deal while other times it sends us into bear mode.

For example, I believe people are healthier when they surround themselves with aspects of nature. Filling my home with plants, stones, driftwood, and sea glass I've collected from various places I've wandered has been central to my healing. The plants in my office connect me to the outside, even when I'm sitting at my desk for hours. But if I walk into your home and you don't have plants, it probably won't impact our friendship very much. That difference doesn't undermine my safety in your home or make me feel like you are a threat to my physical or emotional security.

On the other hand, I hold a core belief that my home should be a safe space for all of us to land at the end of the day. I am a *fierce* protector of this space and have spent years teaching my children how to be self-aware and compassionate, and how to navigate conflict in ways that honor this priority of safety. One of the greatest challenges we faced during the time we fostered Fia was figuring out how to hold space for a traumatized teenager who needed to express her pain but had never been taught how to self-regulate. Our foster daughter was smart, funny, and loving. She didn't hate us, and she never engaged in risky behaviors or put anyone in physical danger. What strained the safety of our home was her expression of overwhelming pain from being in the foster care system and being the child of parents who were consumed by decades of addiction.

If I'm being honest, we butted heads a lot because Fia's volatility challenged many of my core and peripheral beliefs. My efforts to help her fit into our family structure probably felt like an attack on her beliefs and criticism of the parents she was fighting so hard to stay connected to.

While we loved each other, things just kept getting harder because we didn't know how to honor each other's values. As the parent, I also struggled to see that Fia's challenges were part of her dysregulation and very tender spaces, rather than attempts to push me around. It wasn't until months after she returned home to her biological parents that I was able to calm my nervous system enough to understand how much baggage we both brought into the relationship. That realization kicked off a long season of working to reconcile this new understanding with my life experiences.

Reconciling the Old and New

Some of the information you gathered and sorted in the previous chapter will challenge what you believe. Some information will be so radically different from what you were taught that sitting with it feels scary and threatening. The more threatened you feel, the more likely it is that the new information is bumping up against a core belief.

The inner turmoil you feel when the new bumps into the old can be temporary if you wrestle long enough to figure out what's worth keeping and what isn't. This is the reconciling stage of vulnerable exploration.

The *Oxford Advanced Learner's Dictionary* defines "reconciling" as: "to find an acceptable way of dealing with two or more ideas, needs, etc. that seem to be opposed to each other."[1] In vulnerable exploration, reconciling the new information you've gathered with your belief system involves being brutally honest about where there's conflict and where there's compatibility. There will likely be a lot of conflict in this part of the process; the very point of deconstruction is to challenge and sort out the core beliefs that we are questioning.

If the new and old information can't fit together in a belief or belief system, something needs to be released. Sometimes the new information isn't convincing enough to shift an old belief. Other times it's the old information that no longer fits as the basis for a belief.

With peripheral beliefs—that is, the beliefs you hold that inform your overall belief system but are not central to it—sometimes releasing can be as easy as saying the old belief no longer fits and just letting it go. Other times, acknowledging how something is no longer consistent with your understanding will stir up deep grief, require months (or even years) of therapy and coaching to work through, and may even feel like the biggest, hardest thing you've ever done.

Reconciling the information and releasing those old core beliefs requires us to feel all of our feelings. Sometimes we need to grieve the harm we've done under the old beliefs because we didn't treat people fairly. There are also times we need to get really angry that God's word has been twisted to hurt people. Other times we feel deep sadness that no one taught us better because the people who loved us and taught us didn't know any better themselves.

All of those feelings deserve to (and *must*) be felt and released so resentment doesn't build up. Don't avoid the topic altogether. Remember to embrace your own pace, listen to what your body needs, and trust yourself as you reconcile the old and new.

Acknowledging the Cost of Control

On some level, we all have control issues. Either we believe control will keep us safe and are drawn to establishing control, or we believe it puts us at risk for criticism, accountability, or even personal corruption, and we want nothing to do with it. Control is, of course, on a continuum with lots of points between those two extremes. What I've learned in my years of coaching is that the more trauma a person has experienced, the more that person is drawn to one extreme or the other.

My repeated traumas and mile-wide stubborn streak have given me broad shoulders and a strong back that would make Atlas jealous. I gravitated toward the extreme of wanting more control because I thought I was the only one I could trust to keep me (and my loved ones) safe. Perhaps you, like me, tend to cling to hard things because when something painful is locked in our emotional dungeons, it feels like it can't hurt us (or at least we know where it is and it only hurts a little). My fear was that once I opened my death-grip on control, released it into the universe, and stopped watching it, I would also relinquish control of what could happen next. I didn't love that unpredictability.

If you seek maximum control too, I want you to know that it takes an immense amount of trust to turn your attention away from what has wounded you. You can release it. The alternative is to continue to pay the tremendous cost required to push things down and wall off the tender parts of you.

If you have zero problem letting go of control, and actually prefer not to have it, then the hard part of this stage will be reconciling, because you have to take full responsibility for what happens. No one else can get in your head and decide what beliefs and practices deserve to stay and which ones have to go. I want you to know that you are more than capable and ready for this. Even if everyone else has abandoned you, you have your own back and everything you need to do this well.

Whatever your typical response is with regard to control, reconciling and releasing invites you to find balance in how you respond to losing beliefs, community, and relationships with people you thought would always have your back.

Navigating Loss without Creating Resentment

"I'm so glad to be out of that relationship. That person never loved me or cared about what I needed. Instead, they just exploited me for their own purposes. I'm happy it's over, and the only thing I feel is really mad at myself for not ending it sooner."

Does this reflection sound familiar to you? Yes—same for me.

Most of us have been so wounded by an unhealthy relationship that we've said something similar. Many of my coaching clients say similar things about the church or religious community they're pulling away from, and in some cases it's true. But in most situations, I would argue that the statement above betrays an avoidance of deep grief over both what was lost and the way the person speaking was harmed.

When an important relationship goes bad, it's easier to push our grief over what was lost to the back of our minds, wall it off, and rely on our anger to push us through. It's much harder to sit with the simultaneous love and rage we feel for the other person. The feelings seem incompatible.

Sometimes it's easier to change the story to "they never loved me" than it is to navigate the complex grief of being hurt by someone who really did love you.

Resentment requires less vulnerability than reconciling seemingly incompatible emotions and experiences, but it doesn't bring healing. It just creates walled-off sections of emotions and makes it more challenging for us to lower our walls in subsequent relationships.

Deconstruction is similar to working through a bad breakup, because at the core, we are deconstructing toxic relationships with ourselves, our belief system, our religious community, and God. Sometimes deconstruction feels like it's too much to navigate, and we flatten the narrative into one where we were never loved, the relationship was never real, and we are better off now without all of those relationships. This is not the whole story.

Choosing resentment and diverting your attention away from the complexity of your pain won't move you toward healing. Reconciling and releasing is the only way to find deep, lasting healing from your time in toxic religion. The purpose of this stage is to reconcile what you know, what you believe, and what you do while releasing what no longer serves you. This is where the information you've gathered begins to change your beliefs and impact how you live out your everyday life.

Releasing What Doesn't Line Up

Now that you've reconciled your new knowledge with what you believe, it's time to release the things that no longer align with your belief system. Some of the more surface ideas and peripheral beliefs will be easy to release. You may even have released them in the midst of exploring the ideas, thus leaving little work to do now.

While you may be tempted to rush through this stage and assume that thinking "I'm letting go of this" is the whole process, I'm going to ask you to trust me and the process and slow down.

The deeper-seated ideas that are more central to your core beliefs will require more effort to release. You'll want to be intentional about making time for coaxing out any ideas that stir up tender emotions, bittersweet memories, and complex thoughts.

Removing such deeply rooted pieces of your belief system may leave empty spaces that are tender for a significant amount of time. Please be gentle and patient with yourself as you care for those tender, wounded spaces that may have been kept hidden for so long. There's no shame in "feeling all the feels," and you're not doing anything wrong if this is harder than you want it to be. If anything, your tenderness is a sign that you're showing up fully, doing the deeper work, and setting yourself free from all the harmful beliefs you've been carrying around.

Avoid the temptation to reconstruct defensive walls and process your emotions "later," when you imagine you'll be more ready than you are today. Pushing things down the road only makes it harder to deal with them the next time. The perfect time to sit with your pain and complex emotions is right now, even if you feel busy or have people relying on you. You deserve all the space and resources needed to nurture your tender spaces.

When you choose to release an idea or change a belief, offer extra awareness to your body and pay special attention to your feelings. Double down on your commitment to embodied curiosity and vulnerability by checking in with yourself regularly. Grief and anger grow really loud when you start tugging on these deeply rooted ideas.

These feelings (and any others coming up) are completely normal and healthy.

Sit with them.

Experience them.

Let them occupy their space.

Marking This Season with Ceremony

Holding a ceremony to release big beliefs may seem hokey, but there's a reason for having a tradition of symbolic gestures in response to significant moments in life. Whether it's relishing the pomp of a university graduation, throwing a going away party for a colleague, sharing sweet memories at your grandmother's funeral dinner, or hosting a good riddance bonfire at the end of a relationship (fueled by everything that a cheating ex left at your place), ceremonies signify that things are going to be different from that moment on.

Ceremonies focus our attention and communicate to everyone involved that what is happening there is important. Ceremonies quiet the constant phone alerts and bids for attention. The work you've done to get to this point—to be present in this season of releasing what's no longer resonant with your soul—deserves to be marked by a sacred moment dedicated solely to what you need.

Releasing what no longer aligns with your belief system can be as simple or as layered as you desire. You can do this alone or ask a trusted friend or loved one to support you in the moment. Your goal is to create something that serves as a container to hold space for all the emotions that come with major transitions. Your ceremony can last for a few moments or it can be several days long.

So go ahead and hold a wake for the "biblical man" or "biblical woman" you thought you had to be. Burn that old toxic purity culture book. Hold a scream fest in the woods to release your rage over years you lost trying to avoid hell. By symbolically releasing what you no longer believe, you will release yourself from the expectation to be the person you used to be when toxic religion defined you.

9

Recenter On What Is Good

I hope you have spent time recovering after releasing what no longer aligns with your belief system (perhaps by taking a nap or two). At this point, I hope you're enjoying feeling less pressure. You might even feel like you have the bandwidth to make a real change in the world. Perhaps you do, but it's okay to stay focused on your own deconstruction. You're still building muscles that help you set and keep your own pace and you're learning how to lean into vulnerable exploration. I recommend taking a little more time to hone your skills before seeking out a more active role in the world.

For the first time in your deconstruction journey, you will have more space to settle into the beliefs, practices, and relationships that are good for *you* in this season. This point should feel like a welcome relief after the heavy investment of time, energy, and emotions into your deconstruction.

But people who have grown up with the pressure to remain busy doing something worthwhile don't always know what to do with themselves when they suddenly have more space and face zero expectations. Without being intentional about what you do with this newfound space, you risk falling back into old habits. The deconstruction work isn't done yet.

In this chapter, you will learn how to find the balance between *being* and *doing* so that there's time and energy left for more exploring. It's important not to overfill this space with busyness or to slip back into those old habits of being productive, seeking external validation, and walking through the world with tightly closed fists.

Instead, this is the space where you learn how to refocus on what's good, settle into routines to keep you vulnerable and curious, and become familiar with the space you now have to breathe deeply and experience your spirituality. The previous stages were likely really hard, and you were taking a lot of action. This season is less about *doing* all the things and more about getting comfortable *being* in this new posture.

In addition to learning how to navigate the world in this new posture, you will discover that you have more items in your buckets in need of your attention. As I mentioned in chapter 7, you will have *at least* four buckets:

Revisit: Information that you are curious about and want to explore more.

Keep: Information that feels resonant and you want to lean into.

I Don't Know (IDK): Information that you have no idea what to do with right now.

Release: Information that no longer fits and you need to let go of.

There are also more topics and habits that you will want to examine through the vulnerable exploration process.

Remember, deconstruction is a journey that takes a long time. You've spent years (perhaps even decades) in unhealthy religious systems that conditioned you to be closed off and defend your beliefs with all your resources. Now is the time to recenter on what is good.

Considering Recentering

Recentering looks different for each person depending on what you're left with after releasing what wasn't in alignment. If prayer has been the topic you've been working on while learning the vulnerable exploration process, for example, you've likely been deconstructing the patriarchal view from the Old Testament that portrays God as someone who only sometimes answers the prayers of the faithful. You may have sifted out a lot of the unhealthy teachings around legalistic prayer while stuffing down your emotions around always referring to God as an omnipotent, omnipresent male deity who controls your eternal fate.

So . . . what did sorting out beliefs about prayer leave behind in your Keep bucket?

Thanks to your deconstruction journey, you know that you're free to pray in non-legalistic ways and speak from a vulnerable, curious posture. Because of this new knowledge, your prayer time might have a new structure. It might look more like a casual conversation with your grandmother while walking through her garden. Or maybe you feel increased freedom to express your anger at God because you no longer think you have to convince God you're at peace with your situation, no matter how terrible it is.

Think about it for a moment. If you don't have to present yourself as fully confident and certain, you can even question God's existence in your prayerful conversations with the very God you're not so sure about. How wonderfully authentic is that?

The key with prayer (and other beliefs you'll reconcile and release during your deconstruction journey) is that you've eliminated many unhealthy practices and left more space for the ones you've decided to keep. There are more resources you can dedicate to recentering on what is good—the things you find truly sacred and holy. Giving your attention to the good that remains after sorting allows that goodness to expand and take up more space in your life. So go ahead, dump out your Keep bucket and spend a little time exploring what's there!

Determining Whether It's Time to Reconstruct

As we talk about specific ways to recenter on what is good, I want to circle back to the conversation I started at the very beginning of our time together. There's a lot of talk about how essential it is to move from deconstructing your faith to reconstructing it. While there may be aspects of your faith you long to rebuild, much of the pressure you may be feeling to do so is likely rooted in the deep fear of isolation and abandonment. The underlying fear of deconverting and losing everything totally makes sense, because that's what toxic religion teaches would happen if you start down the slippery slope of doubting and deconstructing. Even the most fly-by-the-seat-of-their-pants person relies on stability and structure to feel safe enough to embrace spontaneity. The longing to be part of a community that shares your beliefs can be so strong.

The isolation of deconstruction tends to exacerbate a longing for community. To join most faith communities, you have to know what you believe before you know which group of people you'll fit in with. Reconstruction seems like the most logical choice if you evaluate your next steps through the lens of your old belief system. There's also a *ton* of cultural pressure to fill the empty space you just created with something that's "meaningful" and "productive." For many people on a deconstruction journey, the desire to jump into a new religious community and become champions for the beliefs we now hold feels like the natural next step.

But the entire point of deconstruction is to move away from toxic pressure and from being walled off and wounded, so perhaps something other than reconstruction is needed here. Just because you've taken something out of your belief system doesn't mean you need to rebuild right away or that something new needs to replace the now-empty space.

Think about when a surgeon removes a cancerous mass. It's rare for the surgeon to put something in the space occupied by the tumor; usually, the goal is to remove the mass and allow the body to heal or the organ to perform its job more effectively. Sometimes a surgeon will put something similar in the space where the harmful tissue was removed (like in breast reconstruction surgery), but the function of an implant is quite different from what was removed. The implant is something that helps the patient reclaim a sense of self. In the same way, considering whether or not to fill new space after faith deconstruction is not about trying to fill the exact same role held by the thing you released; you released what was harming you.

Rushing to establish a new belief system, join a new faith community, and embrace the culture immediately often results in disappointment. The replacement will likely fall short of what you hope it will be. It's better to ignore the pressure to reconstruct your faith; you don't need to seek external validation instead of the internal validation you've found along your deconstruction journey.

Recentering on what is good teaches you how to love, trust, and affirm your journey even if no one else does. Recentering is a season of learning how to validate and form deep attachments to yourself instead of relying on a faith community to help you feel like you're on the right path.

Avoiding Overwhelm by Reframing Choice

You're in the "rinse and repeat" stage of deconstruction where you will repeat the process of vulnerable exploration to tackle complex ideas and beliefs. It may be intimidating to think about all the topics you have yet to tackle and all those buckets that still need attention. But even that sense of intimidation is likely rooted in the toxic religion system you are leaving behind. In chapter 5 I talked about how trauma taught you to look for signs that a threat is present so you can quickly figure out how to make yourself safe.

Having or making choices might feel unsafe because you were conditioned to believe that making the "wrong" choice could lead to conflict, shame, or punishment. The uncertainty that arises when it's time to make a choice can be terrifying in this season of questioning. If your history confirms the idea that making a choice is inherently risky, choosing what you want to recenter on in this season may actually push you away from embodied curiosity and vulnerability. To combat this, you'll want to write a *new* story for yourself that focuses on the opportunity presented by having choices, rather than focusing on potential impending disaster if you make the wrong choice.

Disaster posture is held by a person who assumes that disaster and crisis are always looming. And if toxic religion is in your recent past, that sense was true. You are accustomed to standing with one foot in bear mode, which means your nervous system is always a little on edge. Disaster posture is so common in people in toxic religious systems that it might appear to be a normal healthy way to live, but it's not. Those of us who are in the deconstruction community have learned the dangers of constant disaster posture the hard way.

The world appears to be full of threats in disaster mode, so this posture tips the scales in favor of the community instead of your own judgment. When you live in disaster posture, the community appears to protect (or at least offer some buffer against) impending disaster. In bear mode, your body is focused on survival and finding safety, so it's harder to override your biological instincts in order to stay connected to and engage all the parts of your body. You are more susceptible to groupthink and your response to certain stimuli is much more predictable.

When you face a choice that might separate you from your toxic religious community, the weaponization of belonging becomes even more effective. The stakes seem so high for you if you choose to "live outside the safety of the flock." You might have been conditioned to believe that the flock provides safety and that living outside the flock is dangerous. Your body may be locked in a fight over who to listen to. You may walk around with your internal alarms going off about the current misalignment of your beliefs, yet your conditioning tells you to keep hitting snooze and stay in the flock. You may be struggling, but your body and mind have been conditioned to believe that "out there is worse."

Several theologies fit this description in toxic religion: choosing between being lost or saved, going to heaven or hell, and being blessed or cursed. If you make the wrong choices, not only will you suffer during your life on earth, but your suffering will also be eternal—and you will likely drag your loved ones down the same doomed path. So for your own protection and the protection of others, it's best to remain on the paved road your faith community is walking down. Disaster posture warns you not to wander off.

In actuality, disaster posture catastrophizes choice and freedom. It keeps your nervous system activated and encourages you to put your walls up. It can also exacerbate contempt you feel for those who are deconstructing or happily living outside the rules of that particular community.

Merriam-Webster defines *contempt* as "the act of despising: the state of mind of one who despises."[1] The *Oxford English Dictionary* defines it as "a feeling of dislike or hostility towards a person or thing one regards as inferior, worthless, or despicable."[2] I'd be willing to wager that you've felt despised, scorned, and treated like you were worthless when you have shared your deconstruction journey with the people who are still inside your old religious community. I have, and it stings. I hope it helps you to know that their contempt has very little to do with you and instead is their self-protective measure to avoid their perceived threat: choice.

Lately, contempt seems to have become the go-to response for those still living in a toxic religious system. It's deployed against people who choose to deconstruct their faith when shaming, overpowering, and threats of getting kicked out of the community aren't having their intended effect. The recent rise of people promoting Christian nationalism is a master class on how to leverage contempt to send people into bear mode so they'll defend something (in this case, the freedom to practice Christianity in America) that's not really under attack.

Choice isn't a threat to or the enemy of a healthy spiritual life—rather, it's the catalyst for growth.

Opportunity Knocks in the Wilderness

Instead of living in a disaster posture, I invite you to develop a totally different perspective on choice (and really, the world). Opportunity posture offers a perspective to look at every challenge or question as an opportunity to learn and experience something different,

You may not have realized it, but since you opened this book, you've been learning to settle your nervous system, stop catastrophizing choice, and shift into this opportunity posture. It's at the heart of vulnerable exploration. Opportunity posture allows you to enter into this process without assuming from day one that the journey will cause hellfire to rain down on you. It teaches you to withhold judgment until after the experience happens, or at least helps you to develop opinions *during* the experience rather than shutting down any other possibility or perspective from the start.

An opportunity posture invites you to process experiences with your whole body and use your entire tool kit, rather than just those "get safe" tools our body chooses when we move into bear mode.

Before we go any further, I want to be perfectly clear that when I talk about recentering on what is good, I am not advocating for spiritual bypassing, in which a person avoids the pain and heavy lifting done in deconstruction in favor of overemphasizing happy, spiritualized things.[3] Spiritual bypassing is another version of toxic religion, and it is deeply rooted in white supremacy and cultural appropriation of Indigenous practices. To say more requires having a longer conversation on a different day. All you need to know right now is that recentering on what is good is not a defensive tactic meant to hide you from the very real pain in the world. When you recenter, you aren't pretending everything is good and happy. Instead, you are embracing choice and opportunity while trusting your ability to navigate the experience, whatever it is, in a posture of embodied curiosity and vulnerability. You still have access to bear mode if there is legitimate danger; trust yourself enough to reserve it for when your survival is threatened.

Recentering on what's good requires maintaining vulnerability and deep connection to all the parts of yourself—without judging or shaming yourself or others. The opportunity posture encourages vulnerability instead of defensiveness. If you have carried a lot of heavy trauma, this opportunity posture will be a whole different kind of difficulty.

If you are used to operating in the disaster posture, choosing the opportunity posture may make it more difficult for you to release things at first. This is a new and different way of looking at the world, so it will not feel familiar or easy . . . at least, not yet. You will learn to choose to release things because you *want* to, not because there's a crisis forcing you to. This will take time to learn, so be gentle and patient with yourself as you build these new muscles.

There is good news. Because you've been deconstructing and really leaning into vulnerable exploration, your contempt and resentment muscles should be starting to wither. That's a fantastic thing, and it's what you've been working so hard to make happen whether you realized it or not. In the short term, though, it can create a little instability as you transition to a more open-handed stance. When there's no longer an impending disaster, you will feel out of alignment if you try to leverage old defensive tactics like contempt. Each time you embrace choice and opportunity instead, it should be harder to stir up contempt and resentment and to push new people and ideas away if you're being honest about them (and yourself).

Your new muscles of embodied curiosity and vulnerability are still developing, so this whole season may feel wobbly and unstable. It's okay. Give it time. Trust the process and trust yourself. I promise it will be easier the more you do it.

Embracing an Equitable Wilderness

Avoiding disaster posture requires you to partner with all of yourself to explore the wilderness without a sense of scarcity, focus on people pleasing, or catastrophizing every decision. This is why it's so important to recenter on what's good instead of rushing to fill all the new space you created when you examined and sorted your beliefs.

By being here and nearing the end of this book, you indicate your commitment of your personal resources to deconstructing your faith. You're hungry for change. If you compare deconstruction with gardening, this season of recentering on what is good would be considered the time when your plants finally expand, bloom, and produce fruit. Why? Because you did the hard work of preparing the soil, removing the weeds, and nurturing what you wanted to grow. You can see some results—this is exciting!

At the same time, it's really important to acknowledge that your ability to deconstruct, set your own pace, and learn to embrace the wilderness is related to your position of privilege within an imbalanced and unjust power structure.

The more marginalized someone is within the toxic religious system, the harder it is for that person to carve out resources to do this work. People who live under constant threat of harm and struggle to have their basic needs find it harder to calm their nervous systems. People who live within the intersection of multiple marginalized people groups will need different spaces and support systems to deconstruct—not out of weakness or ignorance (don't let white saviorism creep back in), but because toxic religion is built to harm them more than the majority white/cis/hetero/educated people who are in the faith deconstruction space.

We have to place the blame for this perpetuated inequity squarely on the shoulders of those upholding the imbalance of power rather than those who are being devastated by it. As you recenter on what is good, continue to feed what is good and, when you can, offer to hold space for those who are gasping for air under the weight of multiple oppressive systems. (Just be sure you don't deprive yourself of life-giving oxygen in the process.)

Stand up for what you believe in. Challenge oppression. Fight for and alongside people who are marginalized, but don't promote every cause and jump at every chance to be an activist. If you overcommit and attempt to overproduce, you will feed a sense of scarcity. Unjust systems can't be toppled when we exploit ourselves to the point of depletion. It's crucial not to stop here and build a permanent home while trying to make the wilderness more equitable. You'll only end up fortifying yourself with a slightly less toxic belief system that still harms you (and others). Scarcity and hustle are not hallmarks of the wilderness!

Whether you are privileged or marginalized in the hierarchy of toxic religion, it's crucial to give yourself time to simmer instead of falling back into old patterns of shaming yourself into doing more. Vulnerable exploration will create change even if it doesn't happen as rapidly as you want it to. Release yourself from the pressure to make systemic change happen quickly.

Instead of focusing on results, recentering is a season of reconnecting with the parts of you that were not able to flourish inside toxic religion. You have the space and freedom to adopt or create sacred routines that reinforce vulnerable exploration. Now is the time to embrace the liberating practice of making choices with your entire self.

Find the balance between recentering yourself and pursuing equity in the world of deconstruction. We all deserve space to sit in the wilderness and breathe deeply.

Trusting the Wilderness Community

For many who are deconstructing, the church provided a community and a routine for sacred practices. Now that you've stepped away, it may feel like you've fallen into a big gaping hole of isolation, but it doesn't have to stay that way. If you were deeply hurt by your religious community, it may be hard to engage with new people, but you deserve a community to fill your life with joy and connection.

Recentering on what's good includes connecting with the community right here in the wilderness—at your own pace and within the healthy boundaries you've set for yourself. There's an equitability here that cannot be found in hierarchical systems. The wilderness is a fluid space where fellow journeyers can ebb and flow through the seasons individually and collectively.

You don't have to defend what you believe here because the wilderness naturally rejects assimilation and promotes choice. Your exploration is no threat to me, and I celebrate your new discoveries without trying to confirm or refute them. Your flourishing is no threat to my own. I hope you find yourself surrounded by people who feel this way too.

This is a whimsical space filled with Mad Hatters, Cheshire cats, and rabbits in waistcoats leading us on unimaginable journeys. The wilderness is where contradictions unite us in curious conversations and conflicts aren't interpersonal battles we have to win at all costs.

You are in the wilderness, and that is good because the wilderness is always where you were meant to be. The wilderness is not a place you were banished to. It is the place you discover *who you are*. Recentering on what's good will always lead you back to your truest self. Bring all of yourself to every space in this wilderness. Here, you were and are *always* enough. I can't wait to show you how to love and nurture this wild, sacred, and holy *you*.

10

Carry On with Compassion

Throughout our time together, we've talked a lot about how deconstruction isn't a linear process where you start your deconstruction at point A and finish when you get to point B. Instead, deconstruction is an ongoing journey with varying speeds, intensity, and discoveries. Revisiting this truth is foundational for learning to carry on with compassion.

If your initial goal for reading this book was to find your way out of the wilderness because you found it threatening, I hope that you now feel deeply connected to this unpredictable space. Perhaps you even feel energized by the space and have discovered the permission to bring all of you to the table without contorting to anyone else's ideal. It's lovely to finally have room to run.

It would not be fair for me to leave you here, however, without touching on the complex and nuanced ebb and flow of deconstruction. I can say from my own experience that there will be times when you suddenly find yourself revisiting beliefs, relationships, and events you thought you'd completely released. Without knowing why this is happening, people often feel confused, frustrated, and discouraged. Questions about why you are still struggling with a particular issue can trigger you into accepting limiting beliefs around failure and having doubts.

Do not slip back into the old habit of shaming yourself for things you think you should have mastered by now. Having compassion for yourself and for others is rooted in your soul; if you walk around disconnected from your body and a split second away from slipping into bear mode, you just can't access compassion. To create and sustain compassion, you need to remain committed to stay connected to your entire self. This is especially true when you are caught off guard by newly uncovered tender spaces.

Bumping into a topic or belief you thought was fully deconstructed is not a sign of failure, backsliding, or relapse into toxic religion. The opposite is true, in fact. Discovering new layers of old beliefs you thought you'd worked through is a sign that you are leaning more and more into vulnerable exploration. You're trusting yourself to peel back additional layers you couldn't see in previous seasons.

Writing this book uncovered a few very tender spaces for me. I thought I had healed those spaces a long time ago. Even though I was caught a little off guard by the fact that some of these pockets of grief were so raw and untapped, I ultimately realized that this response actually makes sense. I'm a different person than I was the last time I sat in those stories.

After letting these experiences simmer, processing my feelings in my therapy and coaching sessions, and talking through the events with my most trusted inner circle, I realized that self-compassion and healthy boundaries have made all the difference for me. Because I learned to love and nurture myself deeply, my walls lowered a little each day. As my defenses crumbled, they exposed new heartache and loss related to each piece of my story.

The fresh tears I shed over these moments weren't the result of an inner brokenness or weakness that meant I couldn't get through these hard things. They were a sacred sign of the resilience required to keep lowering your walls until the wildest, most sacred version of yourself remains. You can't find this version by trying to outrun your fear of not being enough. The only way you discover who you were always meant to be is by returning to the moments where your needs went unmet and then mothering yourself through the healing process.

Choosing to carry on with compassion means building an equitable relationship with yourself so you value *all* parts of you and make sure they get what they need in the moment. It's time to relinquish your futile attempts to be perfect and give yourself permission to revisit beliefs and ideas as often as you want until they feel right. Learn to love yourself as fiercely and decadently as you deserve.

To do that, you need to let go of your conditioning to please people in order to reduce the chance of being abandoned. Be honest with yourself about what you deserve, and set your boundaries according to your needs, not everyone else's. Maintaining healthy boundaries helps you settle into ease because you won't constantly be taking more hits from people who don't know how to work through their own shit.

It is life-altering to have people who are healed hold space for you. We wouldn't be having this conversation right now without the people who've carved out sacred spaces for *me* to tend to *my* wounds. And I can't find words rich enough to describe the magic that happens when people learn to hold space for their own healing.

How do you do that? Every step of vulnerable exploration has been pointing you back to yourself, and now that you're here, you can turn your attention to learning how to love and nurture the wild, sacred, and holy *you.*

Self-Compassion and Self-Attachment

There are people who spend their entire lives researching attachment; I don't expect you to become one of those people. However, a basic understanding of attachment theory is vital for you to learn how to recenter on what's good without accidentally returning to your old habits of seeking approval.

The American Psychology Association defines *attachment* as "the emotional bond between a human infant or a young nonhuman animal and its parent figure or caregiver; it is developed as a step in establishing a feeling of security and demonstrated by calmness while in the parent's or caregiver's presence. Attachment also denotes the tendency to form such bonds with certain other individuals in infancy as well as the tendency in adulthood to seek emotionally supportive social relationships."[1]

What does that mean? *Psychology Today* calls "attachment" the "engine of subsequent social, emotional, and cognitive development," and it has a significant impact on how we connect with others as adults.[2] When we experience safety and nurturing from our caregiver(s), we form a secure attachment that allows us to learn how to self-regulate in healthy ways. When a caregiver is physically or emotionally absent or relates to a child in unhealthy ways, attachment tends to develop into one of the insecure types: anxious, avoidant, or disorganized.

Your earliest caregivers were your home base and they either helped or prevented you from building the confidence to explore the world in courageous ways. If they created an untrustworthy environment filled with instability, fear, and inconsistency, they taught you the world was unpredictable and dangerous. To survive that kind of untrustworthy world in the safest way possible, you may have learned how to build walls, stay close to home, and fit in with people around you as much as possible to protect yourself.

Healthy attachment to oneself isn't taught by toxic religious communities that need followers to trust them more than they trust themselves. Instead, followers are taught to attach to the community, the beliefs, and the rituals—every bit of confidence that comes from within is labeled as the ego that goes against God's will. Followers are told to die to themselves and never trust their hearts or intuition. As a result, they never learn self-attachment or how being connected to oneself is the key to live an embodied life. Without that connection, they rely on others to tell them what they are worth. If this is what you experienced, you have been conditioned to trust others' opinions more than your own. This leaves you vulnerable to experiencing doubts about your faith deconstruction journey, feeling fear of abandonment, and searching for external validation.

Deconstruction, Attachment, and Mothering

Most of my clients are healers, leaders, and teachers in their own communities. They are generous and compassionate people. They're strong, resilient, and known for carrying heavy loads for others. People around them rely on them heavily, and the ways they're changing generational patterns of dysfunction is obvious to those who know them best.

What is less visible is how much they struggle under the weight of their own pain. They work hard to find peace, but they struggle to find the bottom of their pain and move beyond the fear of abandonment. The very same people who can call forth the best in others struggle to feel worthy and be seen. They work hard to make sure others receive the love they need but struggle to love themselves exactly as they are. What to others seems like a life of compassion and service is often rooted in an exhausting pursuit of love, affirmation, and being or feeling included.

Perhaps you're feeling really called out right now by this description and you feel yourself tip-toeing toward bear mode. It's okay and I understand. Give yourself a big hug, take a deep breath, and remember that you are safe here. Stay committed to your embodied curiosity and vulnerability and keep reading.

The search for external validation is deeply rooted in your attachment style and the attachment style of the people who raised you. The problem with pursuing external validation is that no matter how much you accomplish or how much people love you, it will never be enough to overcome your inability to love yourself. If no one taught you how to love and trust yourself, *actually learning to love and trust yourself* is the only way to heal that wound.

Because your attachment style is cultivated in response to your level of safety in your early years, the good news is that, in most cases, you can change it. Carrying on with compassion invites you to be your own caregiver so you can rewire your brain by flooding yourself with love, safety, and goodness; you can call it mothering yourself. You are literally stepping into the gaps where nurturing was needed most in your earlier years and creating the safety your caregivers were unable to provide.

Mothering yourself fosters strong feelings of safety that allow you to go even deeper into your tender spaces, tend to what was neglected, and recalibrate your attachment style. Moving from insecure attachment to secure attachment recalibrates your entire conversations around relationships with self, others, and your Creator. When your attachment style and behaviors shift, it becomes easier to stop chasing the approval of those who raised you and those you've adopted as mentors along the way.

Mothering yourself is the key to breaking harmful generational patterns and connecting with the version of you that existed before your experiences with toxic religion.

The Mother Archetype

Before we go any further into this conversation about mothering ourselves, I want to acknowledge there may be cultural or experiential baggage related to the idea of a mother. Please set aside the baggage for now and join me in this conversation with embodied curiosity and vulnerability. We will talk about our mothers or the people who took on that parenting role in a minute. But first, we need to define mothering in an archetypal sense that goes beyond our real-life experiences.

Even if you were raised by amazing people, learning to mother yourself will radically change the way you look at the world. Many of us have been conditioned to value the opinions of others over our own, especially when it comes to the opinions of those in leadership positions in our religious communities. This conditioning leaves us highly susceptible to forming codependent relationships where we pursue connection with someone to the point of exhaustion. When we've been taught that relationships with the right person will "complete us," it makes sense to dedicate a ton of emotional and physical resources to finding that person and then making that person happy enough to stay in relationship with us.

Humans are wired for connection. Longing for emotional intimacy is completely normal. It becomes harmful when we prioritize that connection with another person over our own physical, emotional, and spiritual safety or when we are willing to tolerate partners and communities who don't even come close to giving as much as they are getting from us. If we have been taught that a lack of getting our needs meant is our own fault, or that we just need to try harder to earn the love and companionship that we long for, then we end up in unfulfilling relationships that reinforce all of our biggest self-doubts and fears. We neglect ourselves and catastrophize what life would be like if we are rejected by our person or community. If the relationship descends into abusive territory, we might be gaslit into believing the lack of connection is all our fault. Unhealthy attachment patterns could prompt us to double down on our efforts to remain connected to an abuser or abusive community.

In the early twentieth century, Carl Jung, the famed Swiss psychologist and psychiatrist, identified archetypes that were represented both in the inner psyche of humans and externally—that is, within our cultures and communities. Jung proposed that archetypes are both categories we fit into and parts of our hardwired personality that may or may not be expressed, depending on our environment and experiences. One of these archetypes is the Mother, associated with birth, creation, fruitfulness, and redemption (typically in the form of rebirth).[3] Good mothers like the Virgin Mary and Mother Earth are present in our mythology, as are bad mothers like Snow White's and Cinderella's wicked stepmothers. (Notice that "bad" mothers are often categorized as stepmothers, perhaps because we have a hard time assigning the abuse and neglect to biological mothers.)

When I discuss mothering in this book, in my coaching conversations, or on my social media, it's crucial to remember that I am referring to the Jungian archetypal mother, rather than the patriarchal caricature of a mother espoused in toxic religion ("God made women for the primary purpose of having babies"). This caricature harms so many people within Christian spaces. While Jung's work was created in a highly patriarchal society where binary gender was accepted as the norm, I am absolutely convinced that the mother archetype is not limited to women or those who bear children.

Mothering, in its purest form, is focusing one's energy on nurturing, comforting, and providing for the needs of a child who has not yet learned to provide those things. The safety, nurturing, and connection that a mother provides are essential to a person's survival and to the development of healthy attachment. Mothers hold space for children as they learn about the world and become individuals.

Mothering yourself involves rolling back the clock to the season when you relied upon others who were unable (or unwilling) to create safety for you. Mothering is a both/and posture where you are fiercely holding space for your healing while also focusing on sitting in that space tending to your own wounds. In this season of being both the mother and the one being mothered, you are learning to give and receive absolute love that's not limited by mental illness, complex relationships, or generational trauma. The further you move away from toxic religion's twisted beliefs about parenting, the more you will see yourself as worthy of unconditional love.

If you are raising children now (or have some who have grown and flown) mothering yourself gives you a completely new perspective on what it means to be a parent, particularly what it means to parent while being rooted in the abundance of absolute love. In this relationship with self, there's no scarcity around not being good enough to give or receive love. The more time you spend here, the more your fear of abandonment will dissipate because you are learning that you will *always* have your own back.

This season of recentering on what is good is about learning to nurture yourself, especially in the face of the tremendous loss and isolation that often accompanies deconstruction. You're making room to learn how to nurture your tender spaces in ways that the people who raised you probably didn't even know were possible. Mothering invites you to detach your self-worth from the attention and affirmation of others, and recenter on your innate value as a human being. This mothering space is where generational patterns of self-doubt, codependency, and emotional abandonment are broken.

Attachment and Deconstruction

What's particularly challenging about attachment in the deconstruction context is that your early interactions with a caregiver also deeply impact how you treat, value, and care for yourself. If your primary caregiver was unable or unwilling to provide a safe nurturing environment where your basic needs were met, then you may be terrified of abandonment (anxious attachment), stop seeking affection (avoidant attachment), or fluctuate between the two in seemingly random ways (disorganized or fearful-avoidant attachment). This is crucial information for you in this season of recentering. The heart of the vulnerable exploration process is learning how to disconnect your unhealthy attachment to the toxic religious system while learning how to develop secure attachment *to yourself.*

Critics of this book will likely pull the above passage out of context as an example of how deconstruction creates self-absorbed individualists who want to tear down all organized religion and create anarchy. Here is the relevant context: self-attachment is not the same as only focusing on your own needs. Instead, it's an invitation to push back against the constant threats of shame, not being enough, and not trying hard enough to make God (and therefore the community) happy that are so prevalent in toxic religious communities.

There's an even more disturbing side to unhealthy religious communities that we need to talk about. Tightly knit, authoritarian religious communities are breeding grounds for abuse because they teach children to trust the system and the leaders more than their own inner navigation system. No one chooses to be groomed by abusive leaders, and abuse is never the victim's fault. However, there is some data that points toward healthy self-attachment making it more difficult for some types of abuse to occur and continue.[4] Secure attachment makes people less susceptible to some grooming tactics because they aren't seeking external validation with the same level of intensity as those with insecure attachments. When secure attachment is present in people, they are meeting their own social-emotional needs and therefore aren't as easily drawn into relationships with charismatic (but dangerous) people who falsely promise to heal every wound and fill every empty space in their lives.

Forming a secure attachment to ourselves is the key. With secure attachment, we can confidently move around the world in a way that rejects codependent and potentially abusive relationships. Secure attachment to self also undermines others' attempts to weaponize our innate need for belonging; we can resist the pressure to assimilate.

Healthy attachment to ourselves, others, and our Creator is the natural by-product of vulnerable exploration and yields incredible self-compassion.

Self-Compassion Practices

There is a plethora of practices you can use to mother yourself and build your self-compassion muscles. Some will resonate with you in this season and become totally useless in the next; avoid legalistic adherence to any practice and hold space for the ebb and flow of your deconstruction journey.

Here are a few examples of ways people in deconstruction learn to mother themselves with self-compassion:

- Use kind inner and outer language. Words matter, so don't toss them around like they have zero impact on you. When you miss something obvious or flake out about an important meeting, what do you say to and about yourself? Do you call yourself stupid? Irresponsible? Echo hurtful words and phrases others may have spoken over you? It's time to learn a different way of acknowledging your mistakes without self-shaming and self-harming. Don't reinforce the manipulation tactics you've worked so hard to release yourself from.

- Get comfortable with your imperfections. That's right: get comfortable. Why? Because your imperfections are not going anywhere, and pressuring yourself to be perfect only feeds the belief that who you are right now is not enough. Setting the bar to an unattainable height only reinforces your feelings of inadequacy and the predominant culture's pressure to strive harder constantly.
- Learn to love your body as you are *right now*. You've carried a hard load and your body has been with you the whole time. Self-loathing only reinforces the unjust, patriarchal system that wants your body to look and perform a certain way and has no problem exploiting you. Stop trying to become someone else, and learn to look yourself in the eye with love and admiration.
- Stop settling for inequitable relationships. When you work really hard to maintain relationships that aren't healthy, the effort makes it really hard to convince yourself that you deserve better. Move the boundaries to promote your own worth. Start reclaiming the space others are taking up and only invest in relationships with people willing to invest in equitable ways.
- Stay present in and pay attention to your body. Deep breathing, mindfulness, and meeting your body's needs are crucial to feeling safe. Respond to more than the bare minimum signals here. Move beyond reacting to your basic bodily functions and proactively nurture your body in this season.

Mothering Yourself

You are what you need. You've already done a lot of work during your vulnerable exploration to connect deeply with yourself and learn how to settle into your body. Reconnecting with your early, pre-trauma self is a huge part of finding healing, and you've been doing that throughout this book as well.

Mothering yourself is key to this stage of vulnerable exploration because nurturing what's good in you is key to detaching yourself from unhealthy relationships that were established in previous seasons. It's time to go deeper and be more intentional about connecting with and mothering the parts of you that didn't receive the nurturing and safety they deserved. While this may seem like deeply painful work that requires heavy lifting, it will also involve making room for fun, play, and whimsy.

Even if your childhood was relatively secure, or your religious trauma happened later in life, nurturing yourself is vital during this season. Allowing yourself to reconnect with your childhood dreams and hopes will help you move through the grief and loss uncovered by deconstruction without feeling so alone.

I've mentioned mothering yourself as a way to help soften your hurt and care for the deep pain that usually comes with deconstruction. But what you're learning in this chapter specifically is that mothering yourself with self-compassion and infinite love is a crucial step toward cultivating healthy attachment within yourself.

The goal of this season isn't to attach to my opinion of you or to complete a detailed list of all the things you "should" be doing for yourself. Instead, use all the skills you've been practicing in this book to listen to your gut more closely. Because on some level, perhaps buried deep inside, you probably already know what you need, even if you aren't sure whether you have permission to meet that need. Here's the secret that will break your deconstruction wide open: Developing a healthy attachment by learning to mother yourself means *your permission* is the only permission you'll ever need to flourish.

11

Deconstruct without Losing Yourself

Thirty minutes from my home, there's an old convent called Victory Noll that is in its final stages of being used as a sacred space. The property is beautiful and well cared for, but the aging population that inhabits it is dwindling. I always feel a bit of melancholy hovering over the property, and I can't help but wonder what it was like in its heyday.

I've never been inside, but there are several outdoor spots that I've visited when I've felt emotionally spun out or disconnected from myself. I've also taken my kids there a few times to walk the small labyrinth that's tucked in a quiet back corner of the property.

Over the years, I've spent hours walking the path in the twisty circular maze while praying, listening, worrying, and trying to find clarity about some hard things. The labyrinth sits on a hill and is surrounded by a ravine, a line of trees, and the convent. It's tucked neatly into a bowl-shaped space that feels centered; I feel the prayers of previous visitors. The air always feels different here. It's a little heavier, yet somehow I find it easier to breathe. The space is light and hopeful while also feeling anchored and deeply rooted in the past. I'm confident the sacredness of this space is the by-product of being tended to as part of the last earthly home for so many wise, devoutly spiritual women.

It may seem like a strange spot for a mommy/daughter outing, but my youngest child is my road trip buddy, and we both enjoy old spiritual spaces. We've made pilgrimages together to visit grandparents' graves, old churches, and historical sites off the beaten path. So for us, Victory Noll qualifies as a haven to visit when we need to be outside and soak in sacredness.

Last week, my daughter was getting over a cold and not quite ready to go back to school. The weather also happened to be 75 degrees and sunny, and the autumn leaves were at their peak of changing colors. We knew the Noll was calling us, so we packed some snacks, put on some comfy clothes, queued up the latest Taylor Swift album on Spotify, and headed toward the convent.

We made our usual stop en route to visit a local farm to pick up homemade soap and local honey, and then we pulled into the sloping, curvy drive that leads visitors onto the property. There were more vehicles present than I had ever seen, and a handful of construction workers were moving around the property. The blacktop was newly paved, and bright yellow paint outlined parking spaces and curbs.

The normally tranquil property felt different this time. It was still sacred and beautiful, but things were shifting. After an obligatory stop so my daughter could stand under the canopy of her favorite willow tree, she and I made our way to the labyrinth. We passed new signs on the convent building that bore the name of a local behavioral health center. New fence panels edged the parking lot and partially blocked our view of the woods and ravine.

As we approached the maze itself, I noticed the old benches and a few trees had been removed since we were last there. The physical appearance and the energy of the space were shifting, but the space still felt welcoming and familiar. I stepped into the opening of the labyrinth and let my eyes wander down the mulch-covered path. I always pause there to gather my thoughts and decide what I want to focus on as I wander through the labyrinth.

Before I could even ask myself what I wanted to focus on this time, I heard an audible voice say, "There's no need to ponder. You've done that work already." In that moment, I knew I wasn't going to stroll the labyrinth that day. Instead, I was going right to the center stone to anchor myself in the space while my daughter Mary walked around.

I did just that. I walked directly to the center, kicked off my shoes, and sat down in the mulch at the heart of the labyrinth while my daughter walked slowly around the serpentine paths. It's rare for me to be that anchored and connected to myself with another person moving nearby, but it felt easy in that moment.

I had barely sat down when I heard, "You're an immovable force." I knew immediately it wasn't my voice. It sounded like the voices of a hundred grandmothers speaking in perfect synchronization. At that moment, something shifted inside me. I felt invited to release the wandering, pondering, and struggling that defined the last few decades of my life.

A crunchy brown leaf fell from a nearby pin oak tree, floated from left to right, brushed my face and landed softly on the ground next to my left hand. I picked it up and smiled, knowing the left side of my body—the side traditionally connected to feminine energy and mothering—is the side I'd been nurturing the most. It felt as if the breeze was acknowledging the regenerative power of mothering myself and celebrating that I had unlocked the intuitive, creative side of my soul that had been smothered under the weight of toxic religion and multiple traumas.

I silently thanked the trees for their offering and gave my daughter permission to scamper off and climb another one of her favorite pines. I remained in the center of the labyrinth and felt the warmth of the sun on my face. I realized then that for the first time, this wilderness didn't just feel like home . . . it *was* home, and I never wanted to leave it. My season of deep, vulnerable exploration to heal old wounds was coming to an end. I could now turn my attention toward a new season of growth and flourishing.

I've been on the journey of vulnerable exploration for years. I'm still in the wilderness with you. Perhaps when you picked up this book, you thought I could provide you with simple steps to follow so you could get through the wilderness with as few scars as possible. By now, you've probably realized that I am still a work in progress, and simply getting you through the wilderness was never the ultimate goal.

Instead, my goal has been to keep you company in the wilderness. To share my fire when yours may have seemed too small to keep you warm, pass you a heaping serving from my simmering cast iron kettle, and hold space for you under the stars when it felt like your world was imploding—all the while pointing you back to yourself, *because you, my friend, are your own best deconstruction guide.*

Start before the World Is Ready

Vulnerable exploration is good for the world. There may be people who say you're selfish and a heretic for deconstructing your faith, and they won't want to be part of your journey. While it would be wonderful to journey with everyone you know, remember that you aren't deconstructing your faith for them. Stay anchored in yourself as you continue to free the smothered parts of you and untangle from toxic religion.

There will probably be days when deconstruction seems too big to tackle. Before leaving you to continue on your own, I want to briefly touch on where I'd recommend that you focus your energy for deconstruction. This is a long haul and not an overnight shift, so listen to yourself and assess the balance between the internal and external work of deconstruction. There are myriads of individual ideas, situations, and topics to pursue during deconstruction, and on the surface, they may seem unique and separate. But there are seven key areas at the heart of just about every harmful doctrine in toxic religion. Focusing on these will help you uproot everything that's built upon a faulty foundation.

The fact that you've made it this far means you're serious about your deconstruction journey. This is good, because uprooting the false doctrines and limiting beliefs patriarchal religion fosters is deep soul work. It takes heart and courage to challenge what you were taught about God, faith, and yourself.

If you start working on these seven areas (and in this order, if possible), you'll begin to undermine the beliefs that uphold the most toxic religious systems. Again, remember that the goal is to move away from legalism and rigid absolutes, so you may find significant overlap between topics as well as several gray areas.

Deconstructing Self. I suggest starting at the beginning and discovering who you really are without the pressures of toxic religion. "Self" is the lens we look through every day, so begin by asking the question that influences all subsequent questions: "Are we broken, untrustworthy beings forever trying to make up for that thing that happened in the garden, or is there more to the story?"

Key topics to explore: shame, intuition, *ruach* (Hebrew word for the breath of God breathed into humans at creation), gender-specific teachings on self and self-worth.

Deconstructing God. When deconstructing our ideas around God, we dive deep into questions people have always asked, such as "Who is God?" and "What does God want with me?" You'll explore whether God is a strict father figure who wears a MAGA hat and regularly ends conversations with authoritarian declarations like "It's my way or the highway" or just a bogeyman created to keep us in line. You'll also explore whether God is something so much more, different, or fuller than that. Here, you'll get to revisit the expansiveness of the character of the Creator of the universe. You'll study God without becoming lost in legalism, nationalism, and patriarchal chest-thumping.

Key topics to explore: divinity, the Trinity, wisdom, fluidity, the identity of God, and the nature of God.

Deconstructing the Bible. You've probably heard that many Christians believe the Bible is authoritative, inerrant, unaltered, and completely unchallengeable. At the same time, you may find it confusing that there are so many different translations and versions of this text, and you may be confused by strange passages that don't seem to apply to life today. Your task here is to determine whether the Bible is an instructional manual filled with examples of what to do and what not to do straight from God's lips to your ears. Or perhaps you will discover a fresh way to read and revere the Bible as a collection of books shaped by human authors who did their best to represent God's messages.

Key topics to explore: the Bible's history, including where the original texts came from, who recorded them (and what was left out, added, or changed along the way), how the Catholic and Protestant churches settled on their own canons, and how the translation process has changed.

Deconstructing the Church. The western, predominately white church positions itself as the moral authority on all issues and membership in the church as an outward sign of a "good Christian life." In contrast to this image, toxic purity culture teachings, abuse (#ChurchToo), racism, and homophobia reveal flaws. In this area, it's important to dive into who the church was supposed to be and how present-day churches strayed so far from that ideal.

Key topics to explore: the church's authority, connecting with divinity, colonialism, weaponization of belonging, and the relationship between politics and the church.

Deconstructing Power. Tackling this area means challenging the idea that power is equally available to everyone and the resulting belief that those who don't have power (political, economic, social) have *chosen* powerlessness. Loving your neighbors means balancing unjust power systems and creating equitable communities where people can find what they need. In the church, there are prevalent myths about people being self-made and everyone having the same opportunities. This area is where you will explore the intersection of power and religion.

Key topics to explore: racism, misogyny, colonialism, equity vs. equality, capitalism, genocide of Indigenous peoples, and white saviorism.

Deconstructing Bodies. The church's attitude toward bodies (especially female bodies) is complex and often rooted in patriarchy. In this area, you will explore the one thing you can always trust but rarely do . . . your body. You'll dive into the inherent conflict between the belief that your body is a sacred temple, yet we are constantly told that they're also the cause of lust and cannot be trusted. This is the space to explore why Christians spend so much time and energy trying to control other people's bodies and what we should be doing instead.

Key topics to explore: purity culture, sex, lust, embodiment, intuition, ableism and the impact of emotions and trauma on our bodies.

Deconstructing Gender. In this final core area, it's important to challenge the church's loudly-proclaimed belief that being binary is God's way. (Spoiler alert: it's not.) I intentionally save this area for last when I work with clients, not because it's the least important, but because it is the most misunderstood. You'll need to build on what you've learned in the other core areas to understand why the church has traditionally been wrong about gender and how you can choose to do it differently.

> *Key topics to explore:* gender fluidity, the RSV translation of the Greek word *arsenokoitai*,[1] consent, marriage, sexuality, misogyny, and the Trinity.

There's a lot packed into these seven areas, so be sure to give yourself time to explore the topics fully. You'll probably be untangling these ideas from toxic religion for the rest of your life, and that's okay. Just remember to continue deconstructing at your pace; don't let a false sense of scarcity or legalism pressure you.

Keep Going in the Messy Middle

This isn't the end of your deconstruction journey. The good news is that this isn't the beginning either. You've already done some heavy lifting by working through this book. Hopefully you have a clear view of just how harmful toxic religion is, especially when it is transmitted in harmful doctrines and legalism.

Instead of sending you out with trite promises about life only getting better, I want to close this book with a promise. There is more to deconstruction than I've written on these pages. The process you just learned is a tool for you to use as you challenge hundreds, or perhaps thousands, of beliefs you once thought were unchallengeable. Mastering the process isn't faith deconstruction in its entirety, but it will help you tackle racism, homophobia, gender bias, xenophobia, and all the other ways toxic religion hurts people.

Faith deconstruction is a long journey, but you're on your way. I'm proud of you for being courageous enough to admit you don't know what you believe anymore—because that declaration is what opens the door for vulnerable exploration.

I hope that after reading the stories in this book, you also know that you're not alone. From what I've seen, there are tens of thousands of people out here in the wilderness and there is space here for you.[2] You are going to make it, and you don't have to journey alone. There are shoulders to cry on and fires to sit by when the dark night of the soul is long, cold, and threatens to swallow you whole.

In this moment, I hope you remain deeply committed to deconstructing from toxic religion and recovering from the trauma you've experienced.

Healing is hard work, and you are doing it.

You will always have your own back.

You're not in this wilderness alone.

Be abundantly kind to yourself during this journey.

Make time for stillness and movement.

Surround yourself with fuzzy blankets and foods that nourish you.

Remind yourself often that God is big enough to handle all your questions, doubts, and emotions.

The wilderness is also big enough.

So are you.

Keep going.

You deserve to be free.

Notes

Introduction

1. Melanie Mudge, "What Is Faith Deconstruction?," *The Sophia Society* (blog), March 7, 2022, https://tinyurl.com/28mjdhct.

Part One

1. Kyle Chastain, "The Church Is Headed for Another Reformation: All Signs Point to It," Medium, March 7, 2022, https://tinyurl.com/2tmhjaj5.

2. Phyllis Tickle, *The Great Emergence: How Christianity Is Changing and Why* (Grand Rapids: Baker Books, 2012), 30.

Chapter 1

1. I place "2S" at the beginning of "LGBTQIA+" to represent the Two-Spirit Indigenous people who were the first people marginalized for their gender and sexuality in North America. On the *Indian Country Today* website, Tony Enos reports that 2S "is not a specific definition of gender, sexual orientation or other self-determining catch-all phrase, but rather an umbrella term." You can read more at https://tinyurl.com/3jpubw3z.

2. In this book, I use “they” pronouns for God because doing so moves us away from the heavily gendered language of Christian fundamentalism that prioritizes masculinity. To learn more about how pronouns for God have shifted over time, see https://tinyurl.com/yne96z9k.

3. “The Matrix Is a ‘Trans Metaphor’, Lilly Wachowski Says,” *BBC News*, August 7, 2020, https://tinyurl.com/yt8s79d4.

4. Brené Brown’s book *Braving the Wilderness* is a great resource for learning more about how this mindset creates conflict and isolation.

Chapter 2

1. These are all real stories from real people who’ve given me permission to share them here. I’ve changed their names to respect their privacy.

2. See Kristopher Norris, “The Problem Was Always Bigger Than Mark Driscoll,” *Sojourners*, August 31, 2021, https://tinyurl.com/2nj9t3ae; and Julie Roys, “Mark Driscoll Accused of Cult-Like Actions; 24/7 Surveillance, Mandated Authority,” *The Roys Report*, May 10, 2021, https://tinyurl.com/5abf9s28.

3. See Daniel Silliman and Kate Shellnutt, “Ravi Zacharias Hid Hundreds of Pictures of Women, Abuse during Massages, and a Rape Allegation,” *Christianity Today*, February 11, 2021, https://tinyurl.com/2ffbnnx8 and Angela J. Herrington, “Ravi Zacharias Is Not an Anomaly, He’s the Very Common Fruit of the Toxic Religious Tree We Have Been Watering for Centuries,” *Deconstructing Faith* (blog), February 15, 2021, https://tinyurl.com/u3z6fnmf.

4. Tyler Huckabee, “Skillet’s John Cooper: It’s Time to ‘Declare War against This Deconstruction Christian Movement,’” *Relevant*, February 9, 2022, https://tinyurl.com/bddsajhh.

5. Some examples include musicians Lecrae and Lisa Gungor; see Sam Hailes, “Deconstructing Faith: Meet the Evangelicals Who Are Questioning Everything,” *Premier Christianity*, March 18, 2019, https://tinyurl.com/4hwy9ecz.

Chapter 3

1. You can find these and other resources at https://tinyurl.com/3wyb jd8c.

Chapter 4

1. Peter T. Leeson and Jacob W. Russ, "Witch Trials," *The Economic Journal* 128, no. 613 (August 2018): 2066–105. https://tinyurl.com/mrcbs4nv.

2. "James VI and I," National Museums Scotland (website), accessed March 10, 2023, https://tinyurl.com/2baj8tc3.

3. Leeson and Russ, "Witch Trials," 2067.

4. Steve Talbot, "Spiritual Genocide: The Denial of American Indian Religious Freedom, from Conquest to 1934," *Wicazo Sa Review* 21, no. 2 (2006): 7–39., https://tinyurl.com/yyaedyvf.

5. "The Philosophy of Colonialism: Civilization, Christianity, and Commerce," *Violence in Twentieth Century Africa* (blog), February 22, 2016, https://tinyurl.com/2vx8zv4k.

6. "Christianity and Colonial Expansion in the Americas," Encyclopedia.com, accessed on October 3, 2022, https://tinyurl.com/4n9kn4tb.

7. Citti Media, *Why Every Indian Should Remember William Wilberforce + March 1813*, YouTube, 2022, https://tinyurl.com/4jpcbdxw.

8. For more on the subject of white saviorism, see Jo Luhemann, "White Saviorism and Christian Saviorism," Facebook video, March 30, 2021, https://tinyurl.com/4437dddr.

9. Equal Justice Initiative, "Slavery in America: The Montgomery Slave Trade," 2018, https://tinyurl.com/ycktuf5n.

10. Equal Justice Initiative, "Slavery in America."

11. Larry R. Morrison, "The Religious Defense of American Slavery Before 1830," *Journal of Religious Thought* 37, no. 2 (1980): 16–29.

12. For more about these apologies, see E. Dionne Jr., "Pope Apologizes to Africans for Slavery," *New York Times*, August 14, 1985, https://tinyurl.com/yc3uka5d; Shawn Sullivan, "Georgetown University, Jesuits Formally Apologize for Role in Slavery," *USA Today*, April 18, 2017,

https://tinyurl.com/bdd625t9; Agence France Presse, "Church of England Body Apologises for Past Slavery Links," January 10, 2023, https://tinyurl.com/2p8cc5hm; Gary L. Carter, "An Apology for Racism," *Washington Post*, June 21, 1995, https://tinyurl.com/27wzfkz2; and Gregg Brekke, "Episcopal Church Apologizes for Its Role in Slavery," United Church of Christ, October 7, 2008, https://tinyurl.com/2p962kbw.

13. Equal Justice Initiative, "Jim Crow Laws," May 1, 2014, https://tinyurl.com/mpjuxc7a.

14. Henry Louis Gates Jr., "The Truth Behind '40 Acres and a Mule,'" accessed February 20, 2023, https://tinyurl.com/2p8pzth5.

15. Equal Justice Initiative, "Jim Crow Laws."

16. History, Art & Archives, U.S. House of Representatives, "Black Americans in Congress," accessed February 20, 2023, https://tinyurl.com/3uzk5m9r.

17. National Geographic Society, "Black Codes and Jim Crow Laws," July 8, 2022, https://tinyurl.com/ms4akpvt.

18. J. Russell Hawkins, *The Bible Told Them So: How Southern Evangelicals Fought to Preserve White Supremacy* (New York: Oxford University Press, 2021), 54.

19. Deborah McAleese, "Mothers of Children Sent off to Australia Were Told They Were Dead, Inquiry Hears," *Belfast Telegraph*, September 1, 2014, https://tinyurl.com/2p88h8wt.

20. "Gov.ie," Gov.ie § (2021), https://tinyurl.com/2p8v42ny.

21. "Irish Mother and Baby Homes: Timeline of Controversy," *BBC News*, January 13, 2021, https://tinyurl.com/yzvfz85u.

22. "Gov.ie," Gov.ie § (2021), https://tinyurl.com/2p8v42ny.

23. "Christianity and the Holocaust," United States holocaust memorial museum (United States Holocaust Memorial Museum, 15 March 2021), https://tinyurl.com/5eecnew9.

24. Robert Wilde, "The Other Reichs: The First and Second before Hitler's Third," ThoughtCo, October 19, 2019, https://tinyurl.com/37e9aasm.

25. "Third Reich," *Encyclopaedia Britannica*, July 20, 1998, https://tinyurl.com/3f2tc992.

26. Christopher Tatara, "Hitler, Himmler, and Christianity in the

Early Third Reich," *Constructing the Past*, 13, no. 1 (April 2013): Article 10, https://tinyurl.com/68kj4jve.

27. Rich Barlow, "How the AIDS Crisis Became a Moral Debate," *BU Today*, December 3, 2015, https://tinyurl.com/yjhwv5px.

28. Nurith Aizenman, "How to Demand a Medical Breakthrough: Lessons from the AIDS Fight," *Shots: Health News from NPR*, February 9, 2019, https://tinyurl.com/4vjjt2zj.

29. Karen Tumulty, "Nancy Reagan's Real Role in the AIDS Crisis," *The Atlantic*, April 12, 2021, https://tinyurl.com/mw7ad7ks.

30. For more on white Christian nationalism, see Ashley Lopez, "More Than Half of Republicans Support Christian Nationalism, According to a New Survey," *National Public Radio*, February 14, 2023, https://tinyurl.com/2hdjhnak; and Joseph Wiinikka-Lydon, "Dangerous Devotion: Congressional Hearing Examines Threat of White Christian Nationalism," Southern Poverty Law Center, December 28, 2022, https://tinyurl.com/yjymay7h.

31. Daniela Ramirez-Duran, "Exploring the Mind-Body Connection Through Research," Positive Psychology, November 26, 2022, https://tinyurl.com/5yw5apr6.

32. Angela J. Herrington, "How to Deconstruct Your Faith from Purity Culture Trauma," *Deconstructing Faith* (blog), January 7, 2022, https://tinyurl.com/2p8mr3a4.

33. Natalie Collins, "7 Lies That Purity Culture Teaches Women," *CBE International* (blog), September 9, 2015, https://tinyurl.com/bdfedyv9.

34. Timothy W. Jones, Jennifer Power, and Tiffany M. Jones, "Religious Trauma and Moral Injury from LGBTQA+ Conversion Practices," *Social Science & Medicine* 305 (2022): Article 115040, https://tinyurl.com/b6rkymhy.

Chapter 6

1. Karen Hao, "Troll Farms Reached 140 Million Americans a Month on Facebook before 2020 Election, Internal Report Shows 'This Is Not Normal. This Is Not Healthy,'" *MIT Technology Review*, September 16, 2021, https://tinyurl.com/yc3d97ht.

Chapter 7

1. Aj is a friend and client who has generously granted permission to share this piece of her story and to use her real name.

Chapter 8

1. "Reconcile," s.v. *Oxford Advanced Learner's Dictionary*, accessed February 20, 2023, https://tinyurl.com/f3yp3r2a.

Chapter 9

1. *Merriam-Webster*, s.v. "contempt," accessed October 30, 2022, https://tinyurl.com/2ujmvmze.

2. Oxford University Press, "contempt, n.," *OED Online*, accessed March 9, 2023, https://tinyurl.com/52fc9k3t.

3. Diana Raab, "What Is Spiritual Bypassing?," *The Empowerment Diary* (blog), *Psychology Today*, January 23, 2019, https://tinyurl.com/4am8yx4t.

Chapter 10

1. "Attachment," *APA Dictionary of Psychology*, accessed July 17, 2022, https://tinyurl.com/3bys929c.

2. "Attachment," *Psychology Today*, accessed November 10, 2022, https://tinyurl.com/5n6ezyu5.

3. Saul McLeod, "Carl Jung's Theories: Archetypes and the Collective Unconscious," Simply Psychology, May 21, 2018, https://tinyurl.com/2s3mbmzj.

4. Ayşe I. Kural and Monika Kovacs, "The Role of Anxious Attachment in the Continuation of Abusive Relationships: The Potential for Strengthening a Secure Attachment Schema as a Tool of Empowerment," *Acta Psychologica* 225 (2022): Article 103537, https://tinyurl.com/5jj5yxjp.

Chapter 11

1. I'll give you a quick preview here. In 1946, this Greek word in the Bible was incorrectly translated as "homosexual." This translation intensified anti-2SLGBTQIA+ doctrines in the church. You can learn more at https://tinyurl.com/4t6kr36y.

2. There is very little data available for us to know the exact number of people who are deconstructing their faith. Many people choose to deconstruct privately, which makes it difficult to collect data.

Bibliography

Agence France Presse. "Church of England Body Apologises for Past Slavery Links." January 10, 2023. https://tinyurl.com/2p8cc5hm.

Aizenman, Nurith. "How to Demand a Medical Breakthrough: Lessons from the AIDS Fight." *Shots: Health News from NPR*. February 9, 2019. https://tinyurl.com/4vjjt2zj.

"Attachment." *APA Dictionary of Psychology*. Accessed July 17, 2022. https://tinyurl.com/3bys929c.

"Attachment." *Psychology Today*. Accessed November 10, 2022. https://tinyurl.com/5n6ezyu5.

Barlow, Rich. "How the AIDS Crisis Became a Moral Debate." *BU Today*. December 3, 2015. https://tinyurl.com/yjhwv5px.

Brekke, Gregg. "Episcopal Church Apologizes for Its Role in Slavery." United Church of Christ. October 7, 2008. https://tinyurl.com/2p962kbw.

Carter, Gary L. "An Apology for Racism." *Washington Post*. June 21, 1995. https://tinyurl.com/27wzfkz2.

Chastain, Kyle. "The Church Is Headed for Another Reformation: All Signs Point to It." Medium. March 7, 2022. https://tinyurl.com/2tmhjaj5.

"Christianity and Colonial Expansion in the Americas." Encyclopedia.com. Accessed on October 3, 2022. https://tinyurl.com/4n9kn4tb.

"Christianity and the Holocaust." United States Holocaust Memorial Museum (website). March 15, 2021. https://tinyurl.com/5eecnew9.

Citti Media. *Why Every Indian Should Remember William Wilberforce + March 1813*. YouTube video. June 27, 2022. https://tinyurl.com/4jpcbdxw.

Collins, Natalie. "7 Lies That Purity Culture Teaches Women." *CBE International* (blog). September 9, 2015. https://tinyurl.com/bdfedyv9.

Dionne, E., Jr. "Pope Apologizes to Africans for Slavery." *New York Times*. August 14, 1985. https://tinyurl.com/yc3uka5d.

Enos, Tony. "8 Things You Should Know about Two-Spirit People." March 28, 2017. https://tinyurl.com/3jpubw3z.

Equal Justice Initiative. "Jim Crow Laws." May 1, 2014. https://tinyurl.com/mpjuxc7a.

———. "Slavery in America: The Montgomery Slave Trade." 2018. https://tinyurl.com/ycktuf5n.

Gates, Henry Louis, Jr. "The Truth Behind '40 Acres and a Mule.'" Accessed February 20, 2023. https://tinyurl.com/2p8pzth5.

Hailes, Sam. "Deconstructing Faith: Meet the Evangelicals Who Are Questioning Everything." *Premier Christianity*. March 18, 2019. https://tinyurl.com/4hwy9ecz.

Hao, Karen. "Troll Farms Reached 140 Million Americans a Month on Facebook before 2020 Election, Internal Report Shows 'This Is Not Normal. This Is Not Healthy.'" *MIT Technology Review*. September 16, 2021. https://tinyurl.com/yc3d97ht.

Hawkins, J. Russell. *The Bible Told Them So: How Southern Evangelicals Fought to Preserve White Supremacy*. New York: Oxford University Press, 2021.

Herrington, Angela J. "How to Deconstruct Your Faith from Purity Culture Trauma." *Deconstructing Faith* (blog). January 7, 2022. https://tinyurl.com/2p8mr3a4.

———. "Ravi Zacharias Is Not an Anomaly, He's the Very Common Fruit of the Toxic Tree We Have Been Watering for Centuries." *De-*

constructing Faith (blog). February 11, 2021. https://tinyurl.com/u3z6fnmf.

History, Art & Archives, U.S. House of Representatives. "Black Americans in Congress." Accessed February 20, 2023. https://tinyurl.com/3uzk5m9r.

Huckabee, Tyler. "Skillet's John Cooper: It's Time to 'Declare War against This Deconstruction Christian Movement.'" *Relevant*. February 9, 2022. https://tinyurl.com/bddsajhh.

"Irish Mother and Baby Homes: Timeline of Controversy." *BBC News*. January 13, 2021. https://tinyurl.com/yzvfz85u.

"James VI and I." National Museums Scotland (website). Accessed March 10, 2023. https://tinyurl.com/2baj8tc3.

Jones, Timothy W., Jennifer Power, and Tiffany M. Jones. "Religious Trauma and Moral Injury from LGBTQA+ Conversion Practices." *Social Science & Medicine* 305 (2022): Article 115040. https://tinyurl.com/b6rkymhy.

Kural, Ayşe I., and Monika Kovacs. "The Role of Anxious Attachment in the Continuation of Abusive Relationships: The Potential for Strengthening a Secure Attachment Schema as a Tool of Empowerment." *Acta Psychologica* 225 (2022): Article 103537. https://tinyurl.com/5jj5yxjp.

Leeson, Peter T., and Jacob W. Russ. "Witch Trials." *The Economic Journal* 128, no. 613 (August 2018): 2066–105. https://tinyurl.com/mrcbs4nv.

Lopez, Ashley. "More Than Half of Republicans Support Christian Nationalism, According to a New Survey." *National Public Radio*. February 14, 2023. https://tinyurl.com/2hdjhnak.

Luhemann, Jo. "White Saviorism and Christian Saviorism." Facebook video, March 30, 2021. https://tinyurl.com/4437dddr.

"The Matrix Is a 'Trans Metaphor', Lilly Wachowski Says." *BBC News*. August 7, 2020. https://tinyurl.com/yt8s79d4.

McAleese, Deborah. "Mothers of Children Sent Off to Australia Were

Told They Were Dead, Inquiry Hears." *Belfast Telegraph*. September 1, 2014. https://tinyurl.com/2p88h8wt.

McLeod, Saul. "Carl Jung's Theories: Archetypes and the Collective Unconscious." Simply Psychology. May 21, 2018. https://tinyurl.com/2s3mbmzj.

Morrison, Larry R. "The Religious Defense of American Slavery before 1830." *Journal of Religious Thought* 37, no. 2 (1980): 16–29.

Mudge, Melanie. "What Is Faith Deconstruction?" *The Sophia Society* (blog). March 7, 2022. https://tinyurl.com/28mjdhct.

National Geographic Society. "Black Codes and Jim Crow Laws." July 8, 2022. https://tinyurl.com/54t2enae.

"The Philosophy of Colonialism: Civilization, Christianity, and Commerce." *Violence in Twentieth Century Africa* (blog). February 22, 2016. https://tinyurl.com/2vx8zv4k.

Ramirez-Duran, Daniela. "Exploring the Mind–Body Connection Through Research." Positive Psychology. November 26, 2022. https://tinyurl.com/5yw5apr6.

Silliman, Daniel, and Kate Shellnutt. "Ravi Zacharias Hid Hundreds of Pictures of Women, Abuse during Massages, and a Rape Allegation." *Christianity Today*. February 11, 2021. https://tinyurl.com/2ffbnnx8.

Sullivan, Shawn. "Georgetown University, Jesuits Formally Apologize for Role in Slavery." *USA Today*. April 18, 2017. https://tinyurl.com/bdd625t9.

Talbot, Steve. "Spiritual Genocide: The Denial of American Indian Religious Freedom, from Conquest to 1934." *Wicazo Sa Review* 21, no. 2 (2006): 7–39. https://tinyurl.com/yyaedyvf.

Tatara, Christopher. "Hitler, Himmler, and Christianity in the Early Third Reich." *Constructing the Past* 14, no. 1 (April 2013): 40–44. https://tinyurl.com/68kj4jve.

"Third Reich." *Encyclopaedia Britannica Online*. July 20, 1998. https://tinyurl.com/3f2tc992.

Tumulty, Karen. "Nancy Reagan's Real Role in the AIDS Crisis." *The Atlantic*. April 12, 2021. https://tinyurl.com/mw7ad7ks.

Wiinikka-Lydon, Joseph. "Dangerous Devotion: Congressional Hearing Examines Threat of White Christian Nationalism." Southern Poverty Law Center. December 28, 2022. https://tinyurl.com/yjymay7h.

Wilde, Robert. "The Other Reichs: The First and Second before Hitler's Third." ThoughtCo. October 19, 2019. https://tinyurl.com/37e9aasm.

Index